Classic Garden Style

Classic Garden Style
Planters, Furniture, Accessories
and Ornaments

TEXT:
INÈS HEUGEL

PHOTOGRAPHY:
CHRISTIAN SARRAMON

"... a simple plank set into the ground and supported

with pegs, a series of log rolls, twigs woven on to

uprights or willow or bamboo bent into overlapping

arcs will all make delightful rustic borders."

8

104

Garden furniture

54 stone

61 wood

68 concrete and cement

73 cast iron

74 town and park benches

79 wrought iron

82 bamboo and rattan

86 wickerwork

88 Lloyd Loom

91 chestnut, hazel and
    rustic furniture

94 chaises longues and
    deck chairs

98 small folding furniture

101 hammocks

102 parasols

Ornamental features

151 garden buildings

157 statues

160 obelisks and stone balls

162 architectural elements

166 weathervanes and roof
    ornaments

170 animal sculptures

175 garden gnomes

179 fountains

Containers and supports

10 terracotta pots and urns

16 Medici vases

20 stone vases and urns

24 metal planters

29 wire artifacts

30 wooden planters

35 zinc containers

36 plant ladders and stands

38 trellis

41 pergolas, tunnels and
    arbours

46 boundaries, gates and
    screens

Accessories

106 lamps and lanterns

113 garden games

116 aviaries and cages

122 nesting boxes, birdbaths
    and feeders

126 scarecrows and bird-scarers

131 basketry

132 tools

140 cloches and greenhouses

144 watering cans

146 wheelbarrows, carts and
    trolleys

52

148

terracotta pots and urns

Medici vases

stone vases and urns

metal planters

wire artifacts

wooden planters

zinc containers

Containers and supports

plant ladders and stands

trellis

pergolas, tunnels and arbours

boundaries, gates and screens

terracotta pots and urns

From modest little pots to enormous glazed urns, terracotta is the garden designer's indispensable ally. The colour of the clay, the techniques, skills and traditions of the potter's craft — practised throughout the Mediterranean since the Stone Age — vary from country to country and one locality to another. Clay worked in Italy, for instance, has a beautiful dark rose hue, that found in Spain is more of a pale straw colour, in Greece it is a sort of powdery white, while Portugal is renowned for its vibrant glazes. In France, the southern regions bordering the Rhône produce glazed earthenware in ochre, brown, yellow or green, the Auvergne offers modest and austere variations in black, green and dark red, while the north is noted for stoneware.

Throughout Europe there are a number of centres with centuries-old traditions of making pots and vases especially adapted for the garden. A prime example is Biot, the home of the storage jar. In the 1400s, sixteen Genoese families took up residence in this small town in the Alpes Maritimes, near Nice, and began manufacturing jars for storing oil and grain. They also made *bugadiers* — large pottery vessels for boiling water for washing. Their technique used a rope-driven wheel, which allowed the potter to work the heavy clay to throw vessels of considerable size, and from the sixteenth century onwards, the necks of these pots were glazed. Destined for cellars and storerooms, these shapely storage jars were round, oval or wide-bellied at the base and capable of withstanding frost and inclement weather.

In 1610, a group of craftsmen installed themselves in Anduze, a small village on the edge of the Cévennes. Their speciality was decorative frost-proof pots that were designed for exterior use. These potters began to trade with Liguria, in Italy, and it was there that they probably encountered the Medici vases and, from the seventeenth century, they began to add a foot to their pots, decorating them with coats of arms and swags. They applied

TOP LEFT
Large terracotta urn with ribbon and tassel decoration and flame finial.

TOP RIGHT
The appeal of these Spanish pots derives as much from their shapes as from the irregular coloration.

OPPOSITE
A huge storage jar, with powerfully rounded sides, stands on guard under an ancient gnarled tree.

LEFT
*A collection of simple
terracotta pots given
a mock-classical patina.*

COLLECTING TIP
*The value of ancient pottery
depends on its condition and
damaged glaze, cracks and
amateur repairs will all
detract from it. Today, some
pieces are artificially aged,
so be careful. Authentic old
pots often bear neither the
potter's name nor the date of
manufacture, but sometimes
you will find a symbol like a
Maltese cross or a fleur-de-
lis, a monogram, or similar
device. Other potters signed
their work with decorative
medallions and dated them.*

liquid clay called *slip* to create a beige background, on to which was splashed streaks of colour, green on the escutcheons and brown on the swags. The glaze was produced by lead oxide that vitrifies during firing at up to 1,000°C/1,832°F. For three hundred years, the potters of Anduze have passed their secrets from generation to generation, the only concessions to modern times being the mechanisation of their wheels and the introduction of gas kilns.

In 1620, potters set up business in Aubagne, outside Marseilles, near the Saint-Zacharie quarry where the clay is of exceptional quality. They specialised in vessels for transportation and storage – jars for olives, water or wine. Their expertise was quickly recognised, and they began to export their elegant wares to Italy. The pots were usually monochrome with a translucent glaze and decorated with cabling, garlands and fluting. The number of potteries gradually increased until, in the 1800s, no fewer than 65 were in production. Output seriously declined in the twentieth century, but the potters of Aubagne still maintain their traditions today. The quality of the work is outstanding and they reproduce classical designs in varied tones of blue, honey, turquoise, almond green and white.

However, the sturdiest pots and jars come from Impruneta, a small Tuscan town situated not far from Florence, where high quality clay is available. A centre for potters since Etruscan times, a guild was instituted here as early as 1308. Impruneta produces tiles (like those used on the Duomo in Florence) and pots which will resist frost down to −30°C/−22°F. The local clay is nicknamed *terra turchina*, which means blue earth, because of its high iron oxide and calcium carbonate content. Pots are produced in a range of sizes, with their smooth sides sometimes decorated with festoons and garlands.

TIP
*Terracotta can be cleaned
with soapy water.
It is not possible to guess
whether a pot is frost proof
or not; the most fragile
pieces are those made of
very porous clays, while
those with a bung have
better resistance. If in doubt,
bring them inside in winter.
Another solution is to wrap
them in straw kept in place
with a plastic bag or
something similar.
To mend a crack or break,
apply cement or mastic and
smooth it with clay or sand.
To give a new pot a naturally
aged look, smear it randomly
with milk or yoghurt to
encourage the growth of
moss and lichen.*

OPPOSITE AND OVERLEAF
*Straight sided or flared,
with wide or narrow necks,
decorated or plain, with or
without planting, terracotta
pots have graced gardens
and patios for centuries.*

Medici vases

In the sixteenth century the Medici family stumbled across a gracefully curving vase on a truncated pedestal, its bowl resembling an ancient Greek *cylix*. Made from metal, it dated from the latter half of the first century BC, and was inspired by the neo-Attic vases made in Greece some 400 years earlier. On its sides sculptures depicted the preparations for the Trojan War, and the sacrifice of Iphigenia. Captivated by its elegance, the Medici had it reproduced for the gardens of their many villas, including the Villa Giulia near Rome. In the following century, French artists residing at the French Academy in Rome discovered the Medici vase and copied it in their turn. These copies were destined for the mansions of France, with the most elaborate versions created for the gardens of Versailles and Marly. The Medici vase inspired the finest artists such as Claude Ballin, to create versions in marble, bronze, lead and stone. They were decorated with gadrooning, Greek key patterns, garlands, chimeras, sphinxes and dragons, as well as mythological and battle scenes, and they lined the avenues of royal parks by the dozen.

Two thousand years have passed since the creation of the original vase, and four hundred since the Medici Vase, as it came to be known, went on to conquer the gardens and parks of the world. And there's no real reason it shouldn't go on forever. But to see the original, visit the Uffizi Gallery in Florence, where it remains on display.

COLLECTING TIP

Many modern manufacturers produce Medici vases in metal. Some even leave the factory already weathered, so beware of anything being passed off as an antique. Originally sold by the pair, single Medici vases never fetch as much at auction.

BELOW

Examples of Medici vase designs from an 1897 catalogue of the Société des hauts-fourneaux, fonderies et ateliers de construction, Tusey (Meuse).

OPPOSITE AND OVERLEAF

The elegant Medici vase, whether in terracotta, metal or stoneware, has retained its essential shape for two thousand years.

stone vases and urns

BELOW AND OPPOSITE
Vases made of sculpted stone were all the rage in the eighteenth century. The designs shown here include urns with lids, a pot full of flowers and a basket of fruit.

From the gardens of the Villa Balbianello on Lake Como to the terraces of Powis Castle in Wales, from El Retiro near Malaga to the Chateau of Brécy in Normandy, stone urns and vases are used to emphasise changes in level, lead the eye into perspectives, line flights of steps and dominate balustrades. Their graceful symmetrical curves, combined with statuary and fountains, form a delightful combination in the traditional European garden. Stone harmonises well with vegetation; it develops a delightful patina and, with time, an encrustation of lichen and moss. Some types of stone are decidedly more impressive than others – marble in particular, with its hard, veined texture. This is the white stone of Greek temples and Roman statues, it was used in the gardens of the Italian Renaissance and for the fountains of Versailles. Closely approaching marble in popularity is granite, equally durable and occurring in a range of subtle pinks and greys, to a lesser degree it also inspired the work of sculptors. But from the fifteenth century, Alberti, an Italian design theorist, was recommending limestone for vases and urns. In his view, limestone harmonised more sympathetically with plants and flowers than marble or granite, which he considered too cold. The availability of this material has made it the uncontested star of garden ornaments. Found from Istria in Italy to Portland in Dorset – by way of deposits in the Île-de-France and Burgundy – every type and variety of limestone has lent itself to sculpture.

There is a subtle difference between a vase and an urn. The urn was used in antiquity for collecting water and as a repository for the ashes of the

COLLECTING TIP
Always check there are no cracks as exposure to frost can cause a cracked pot to shatter. For the same reason, never leave water in the bottom of a stone pot during winter.
Granite is a very solid material, but once polished it will not acquire a patina and always looks new, which can be a disadvantage in the garden.
Pots made from reconstituted stone lack aesthetic appeal when new, but, like those made from natural materials, they will quickly grow lichens and mosses, and become indistinguishable in time from the real thing.
It is well worth scavenging around the yards of salvage companies for unusual containers. You may come across water tanks, well heads, tubs, farm feed and water troughs, mortars, mangers, church fonts or stoups, and so on.

LEFT

This group of ornaments in an informal but pleasing arrangement comprises a mortar, a rectangular trough, a pineapple finial and a classical statuette.

BELOW

From the mid-eighteenth century, reconstituted stone was often used instead of the real thing. Less costly, it still acquires the same patina with age.

dead, and usually describes a large container with a lid. Vase is a more general term and the most common form since the Renaissance is the Medici vase (see page 16), which has been reproduced in an infinite variety of styles and adorned with handles and lids. The beauty of its curving lines is such that it does not even require planting, though sometimes these vases are filled with sculpted flowers and fruits. As for its surface decoration, the effects can be quite stunning. During the Renaissance, the principal decorative features were swags and mythological scenes, elements brought to the ultimate degree of perfection in France during the 1600s. The century that followed was dominated by the elegance of the rococo style with its asymmetrical compositions and swirling rhythms.

From the end of the nineteenth century, new shapes and new objects began to replace the vase, which was beginning to be seen as somewhat unoriginal. Instead, water cisterns, barrels, washtubs and sculpted sarcophagi — containers resembling small coffins — began to make their appearance in the garden.

TIP

To clean stonework which has become encrusted with grime, soak it in a dilute ammonia solution, 1 part by volume of water to 2 of ammonia, and then brush vigorously. To restore faded colours, rub lightly with a mixture of linseed oil and turpentine. You can buy commercial waterproofing products which give increased protection against frost.

RECONSTITUTED STONE AND CEMENT

After 1760, reconstituted stone, also known as 'composite', began to rival the real thing. In the 1800s, short-run production of objects made of this cheap material allowed the middle classes to buy ornaments imitating those found in aristocratic gardens. Composite is an artificial stone composed of marble dust or chippings mixed with cement. When poured into wooden moulds, it assumes the form and decorative features of the real thing. They were manufactured throughout Europe; particularly in Italy, France, where numerous designs were advertised in mail order catalogues, and England, where two popular varieties called Chilstone and Haddonstone were produced.

On large estates, craftsman otherwise employed on construction work such as steps and balustrades often made cement vases on the spot. Others were factory-produced and sold singly.

TOP
A pair of cast-iron planting bowls dating from the late 1800s.

BELOW
Cast-iron vase with handles in the form of salamanders.

metal planters

TIP
Lead is a heavy, soft, and stable metal. When exposed to the atmosphere the surface is transformed to lead oxide, which protects it from more penetrating oxidation. To clean lead, use turpentine or white spirit and rinse well.
Painted cast iron requires little maintenance apart from an occasional wash. To renovate a cast-iron vase, first clean it vigorously with a wire brush. Then rub with a pad soaked in undiluted deoxidiser. Leave this to work for two hours, then rinse and dry. If you want to paint it choose a rust-resistant metal paint. If you are unhappy with the appearance of a new iron vase, do the opposite – apply an oxidising product.

COLLECTING TIP
Lead or iron ware from the seventeenth and eighteenth centuries is becoming rare and consequently very expensive. Today the market is being swamped by copies but contemporary pieces are somewhat lighter and are welded rather than riveted. For the most part their designs lack originality.

There is evidence of the use of lead in Eastern Europe since earliest antiquity. The Greeks and Romans used it for water pipes and in their building construction. In the Middle Ages, the stained glass of cathedral windows was set in lead frames. But it wasn't until the seventeenth and eighteenth centuries that the material began to be employed on a large scale in the decorative arts, especially for garden vases and urns. Able to withstand harsh weather conditions, it gradually acquires a silver-grey patina which blends in well with natural surroundings. In the gardens at Versailles and Marly, some of the large Medici vases, decorated with swags of leaves or mythological subjects, are made of lead. The metal was either left bare or gilded.

From the start of the nineteenth century, with an increased interest in metalwork, lead came into its own. It was cheap, and could be painted in bright colours or disguised to look like stone. On the other hand, for so-called ornamental features, it took second place to cast iron. Foundries throughout Europe manufactured countless version of vases, bowls and planters in painted cast iron, reproducing every historical form and style – classical, Renaissance, Louis XV, rococo – and decorated them with a simple frieze or an embryonic form of more sophisticated patterning. In Victorian England, cast and wrought iron became inescapable features of the garden.

OPPOSITE TOP
Wide-bellied metal vase from the late 1800s.

OPPOSITE BOTTOM LEFT
Large metal container imitating the form of a classical storage jar.

OPPOSITE BOTTOM RIGHT
Nineteenth-century wrought-iron basket inspired by the Medici vase.

DOUBLE PAGE OVERLEAF
(left) Lead jardinière with rose decoration.
(right) A collection of cast-iron planters from a late nineteenth-century French funerary catalogue of the Société des hauts-fourneaux et fonderies du Val-d'Osne.
(top right) Interpretation in metal of a shallow flared bowl with handles.

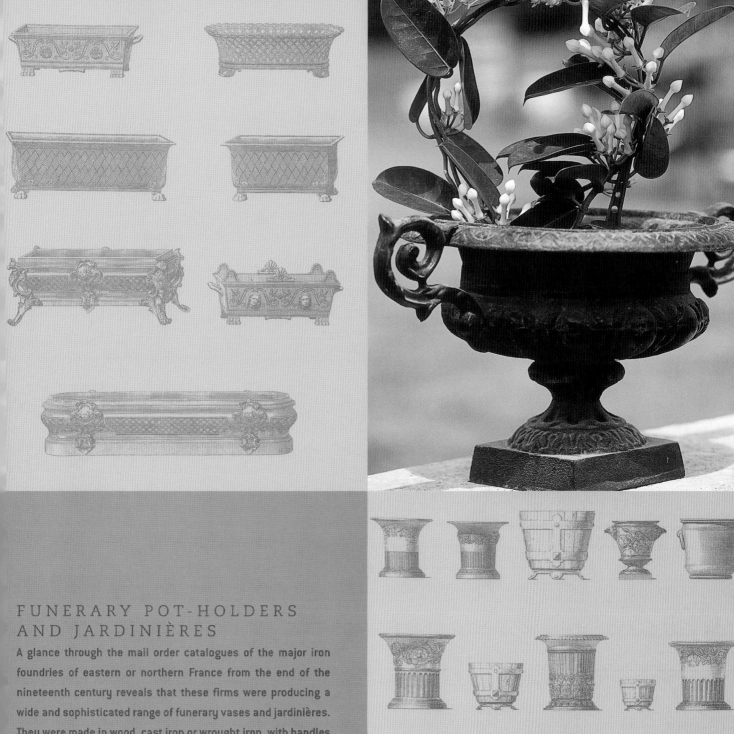

FUNERARY POT-HOLDERS AND JARDINIÈRES

A glance through the mail order catalogues of the major iron foundries of eastern or northern France from the end of the nineteenth century reveals that these firms were producing a wide and sophisticated range of funerary vases and jardinières. They were made in wood, cast iron or wrought iron, with handles or rings, some with feet and others unmounted. Most are characterised by their skilful decoration imitating basket weave or the leading of church windows while human figures appear much less frequently and are used more discreetly than on other types of decorative vases.

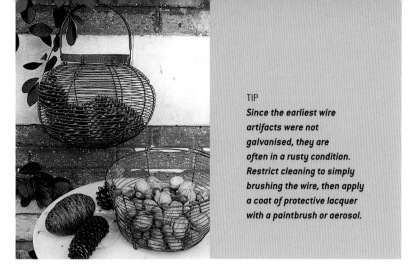

TIP
Since the earliest wire artifacts were not galvanised, they are often in a rusty condition. Restrict cleaning to simply brushing the wire, then apply a coat of protective lacquer with a paintbrush or aerosol.

wire artifacts

OPPOSITE
This unusual structure resembling the Eiffel Tower is made of wire and wire netting. It has three levels for growing alpines.

TOP
Old wire salad baskets are in great demand today and are useful for holding collections of small items.

Handmade wire artifacts form another group of decorative bygones. Wire baskets were once used as containers for fruit, eggs, salads or shellfish, or for carrying drinking glasses or wine bottles. Today they look delightful hanging in the garden, or as lightweight containers. Simply add a moss liner or concealed pot and let wild flowers and plants spill down through the spaces.

The craftsmen who made these objects were originally pottery repairers from Slovakia. They began to use their skills to make domestic utensils and to travel, first to Russia, Germany and France, before crossing the Atlantic and spreading their knowledge throughout America. There, after initially producing utilitarian objects like sieves, baskets and traps for vermin, they moved on to more sophisticated work, fashioning bowls, vases, toys, baskets and bottle carriers. By the beginning of the twentieth century, a thousand or so craftsmen were in business. Numerous workshops opened to supply the large stores; they issued catalogues, and also sold their products door to door. Their designs became more and more sophisticated as each workshop tried to outdo the others in skill and originality. Some artifacts were subtly woven to resemble wickerwork, others matched the level of decoration seen in wrought-iron baskets, yet others imitated braiding, with pompons and spirals. For big occasions, such as a wedding, private individuals would place an order with a craftsman, for whom it was a matter of honour to produce a masterpiece. As a result, wire candelabra, chandeliers and ornate baskets — with some of the work so delicate it resembled lace — were proudly displayed in people's houses and passed down from generation to generation. The fate of the more everyday objects was to be discarded after serving their purpose. Even if tinned, as was sometimes the case, these items gradually rusted and eventually iron was abandoned in favour of more durable materials such as stainless steel or plastic. The last workshops closed their doors at the start of the 1900s.

COLLECTING TIP
The countless wire utensils produced in workshops at the turn of the nineteenth century were not made to last – they would have been thrown away at the first signs of corrosion. This explains why they are becoming increasingly difficult to find. Always consider the condition, workmanship and rarity of the piece before you buy.

wooden planters

TIP

Unless a wooden jardinière is made from a tropical rot-resistant species, it should be taken inside during the winter. There are eco-friendly commercial products designed to protect wood against the effects of damp and you can safely apply these to your tubs. If you use decorative wooden containers in place of urns, don't leave them outside too long; they will stand up to the odd shower but not to a very wet season.
It's best to plant into a plastic container placed inside the tub to prevent the wood rotting on contact with the soil.
Always use a watertight inner container when using a wooden planter for displaying cut flowers.

The first wooden planters appeared in the 1600s. They were designed to hold orange, lemon and palm trees as well as other exotic plants. These trees, because of their dependency on warmth, were brought out into the garden in summer and returned to glasshouses or orangeries for the winter months, except when required to grace some special event or celebration. The Orangery at Versailles, constructed in 1685 by Louis XIV, held over 1,200 exotic trees each in its own wooden container. The advantage of wood over stone is its comparative lightness — making it easier for the containers to be transported on trolleys or mounted on castors. Usually made of oak, they might be shaped like a drum, though the most common design was a square box mounted on feet, with the occasional addition of a finial at each corner — a design that has come to be known as the Versailles tub. To allow the soil to be changed more easily, some containers have a sliding wall that is held in place by metal or wooden bars.

In the nineteenth century, flower tubs were invariably made of oak, with a tar coating on the inside to prevent contact with the soil, which would rot the wood. You can also find examples in varnished beech, and tubs constructed of varnished heart of oak, encircled with metal bands and with handles bolted on. Other types had decorative crowns and a small basin on cast-iron feet to protect the wood against damp and retain any spilled water. In the late 1800s, the importation from the Far East of rot-resistant species, such as teak and iroko, led to the production of planters and garden furniture on a massive scale. The wood was simple to maintain and did not require removal indoors during the winter.

TOP

The Orangery. A gouache by J.-B. Hilaire dated 1794.

BOTTOM

These wooden containers were originally used to harvest grapes.

OPPOSITE

(top) Tropical palms planted in tubs could easily be brought indoors for the winter. This tradition began in the eighteenth century when increasing numbers of exotic plants were brought back to Europe.
(bottom) Wooden tubs form a contrast of materials with the stone trough and two sphinxes.

OVERLEAF

Huge baskets made of woven chestnut wood, and filled with aquatic plants, emerge from the tranquil water of a pool.

zinc containers

OPPOSITE
A simple zinc bathtub left to collect rainwater reflects the blue of the sky.

COLLECTING TIP
A great deal of pleasure can be derived very cheaply from collecting zinc containers. If you want to use them, check that the metal is not full of holes, which means they are irreparable. A holed container or watering can may seem useless, but on the other hand you have an excellent planter for a small-leaved ivy, some pansies or a few daffodils. The holes will let excess water escape.

Zinc has become very fashionable. It is a white metal which, in a dry atmosphere, resists rust. In the damp, it forms a surface layer of hydrocarbonate, which protects it from further corrosion. It is light, and its attractive silvery grey colour – which deepens with time as the patina develops – harmonises wonderfully with the green of vegetation and sets off the colours of adjacent flowers. Like terracotta pots, zinc containers produce a more spectacular effect if arranged in groups or rows.

Though zinc has been known for thousands of years, particularly in China, and a fountain with a zinc crown has been discovered intact at Pompeii, it was not worked regularly until medieval times.

Then, in the eighteenth century, Daniel Dony, a chemist from Liège, invented the first industrial process for making zinc sheet. The English and Americans put this to use on a grand scale, particularly for galvanising iron for use as roofing on buildings. In Europe, in the 1800s, zinc began to be used in the manufacture of all sorts of everyday objects for the house and garden: milk churns, basins, wash tubs, cisterns, pitchers, baths, troughs, buckets, watering cans and every kind of cooking utensil. Many of these unassuming zinc items, used daily by our ancestors, have now been unceremoniously tossed aside in favour of plastic.

TIP
To clean zinc, brush vigorously with warm, soapy water. If the object has acquired a greenish tinge, apply a liquid algaecide, then rinse very thoroughly and leave to dry. To give zinc back its original sheen, rub with fine steel wool. Finally, apply a satin-finish or gloss lacquer.
If you decide to grow plants in a zinc container, first pierce drainage holes in the bottom. It will help to protect the inside if you paint it with a layer of bituminous emulsion; allow it to dry well after application. Line the container with clay balls and fit a circle of thick felt, old carpeting or a piece of blanket before filling with soil.

plant ladders and stands

TIP

Cast iron can be cleaned simply by scrubbing hard with soapy water. For a ladder made of iron and wood, wash first, then sand the metal parts with glasspaper, apply a rust protector, then a coat of beeswax or an oil-based paint. Sand the wooden parts, then either paint them with undercoat and two coats of paint or varnish them, rubbing down with steel wool between coats.

In the past, plant ladders were used mainly in commercial orangeries or glasshouses, allowing visitors or purchasers a clear view to admire large displays of plants in full bloom. They were constructed of various materials – some simple, lightweight examples were made in wrought iron, sheet metal or even wire. Sometimes the frame is metal with the steps made from wooden planks, others are made entirely of metal. In the nineteenth century some very fine models, heavy and sophisticated in design, were available from mail order catalogues.

Plant ladders come in many forms, straight for placing against a wall, circular for surrounding a tree, semicircular, angled or pyramid-shaped. Most have between three and six steps. A few, however, could reach right to the top of a greenhouse wall and held hundreds of pots, so that the flowers cascaded down with majestic effect. In the 1800s, jardinières mounted on legs fulfilled roughly the same function as plant ladders, but were sold to private individuals for their verandas and winter gardens. They were smaller, made of wood, iron or wire, and more elaborately constructed.

Another way of showing off potted plants is to place them on a stand. Plant stands were made of wrought iron, bamboo or rattan; they leaned against – or frequently were attached to – a wall. Often they would imitate a tree or a vine with each branch equipped with a projecting circle of metal or other small support to hold a flowerpot.

TOP
English wrought iron plant stand designed for use in an orangery.

BOTTOM
Plant stands in painted cast iron.

OPPOSITE
(top left) Gourds can be preserved in a simple and attractive fashion by stacking them on the steps of a plant ladder. (bottom) An old wooden box tray on a stand is used to display a group of potted plants.

COLLECTING TIP

*If you come across a
cast-iron plant ladder,
check carefully that it
hasn't had a break repaired
at some stage which may
mean it is liable to have
been seriously weakened.
Similarly, if iron ladders or
display stands have rusted
badly, make sure they are
still solid enough to carry
the additional weight of pots.
Jardinières made of wire can
become unstable, and
bamboo or rattan should be
examined for damage.
In the garden itself, a plant
ladder can be improvised
from a flight of stone steps,
a stool, or a step ladder with
wooden planks placed
across the rungs.*

trellis

TOP
Wall-mounted trompe-l'oeil treillage.

BOTTOM RIGHT
Designs for trelliswork vases dating from 1775.

OPPOSITE
(top left) An intimate little trelliswork retreat.
(top right) An elegant screen is created using wood framed trellis with finials and low box hedging.
(bottom) Living willow woven in a diamond pattern to create a delightful natural trellis.

COLLECTING TIP
Trellising available commercially consists of wooden latticework assembled in squares with sides measuring approximately 15 cm/6 in. It usually comes ready to erect, with the laths nailed together and fixed to stouter side frames. Trellis is often painted green to harmonise with foliage. Make sure any trellising you buy has been treated with plant-friendly preservative.

Trellis or treillage derives from the French word *treille* meaning a supported vine to cover an open space. It is a lightweight latticework of wooden, metal or plastic laths arranged in various patterns – squares, diamonds, fan-shapes, herringbone, and so on – organising and giving structure to different parts of the garden as well as serving as a support for climbing plants. From the frescoes at Pompeii, we learn that the Romans had a taste for this form of garden art, and some editions of the fifteenth-century book *Roman de la Rose* contain illustrations of small, decorative screens that enclose medieval parterres. In the seventeenth century, Le Nôtre, designer of the gardens at Versailles, produced plans for treillage features that were a masterpiece of sophistication. His talent, combined with the public taste for architectural gardens, sparked off a general passion for arbours, porticos, pergolas, arches, festoons, tunnels, gateways, screens and even belvederes and furniture all made of lattice. From the eighteenth century, such features were also employed to lend false perspectives to blind walls, enhance the illusion of space and mask domestic outbuildings. But these simple structures, whether attached to walls or freestanding, were also an excuse for growing climbers such as roses, wisteria and clematis, or vegetables like peas and beans. Treillage can be flat or three-dimensional, but a notable variety of the form is to be found in Dutch gardens, in the shape of obelisks, columns and piers. In Japan, the traditional material for trellis is bamboo, often arranged parasol-fashion with the spokes supporting the branches of flowering cherries.

Traditional trellis is constructed from all kinds of wood. Oak is the most solid, and is used principally for the frames. Hazel, chestnut, ash, elm, cypress, laurel, pine and willow are also common. Wooden laths sunk into the ground are bound together by iron wire; iron is also used for the supports reinforcing arches. Sometimes painted or gilded wrought-iron decorations, in the form of garlands, bouquets or leaves, add a finishing touch to the structure.

pergolas, tunnels and arbours

These lightweight garden features, primarily designed to support climbers, provide welcome areas of shade in summer and make superb decorative features all year round. The word pergola is Italian in origin and means an arbour. It derives from the Latin *pergula*, something projecting or over-hanging. A pergola can be attached to a building or consist of a series of independent columns supporting beams that form an open roof. Both types are designed to support a vine or climbing plant. This must be one of the earliest forms of garden feature; it is known to have been in use in Ancient Egypt, as well as by the Greeks and Romans. The oldest Egyptian pergolas consisted of roughly shaped pillars, but as one dynasty succeeded another, they became more and more elegant, painted in various colours or acquiring sculpted decoration. But the basic structure of the pergola has changed little, even if the supports are made from different materials — wood, brick, metal, stone — and the roofs, whether ironwork, wood or trellis, assume a more rounded form. After all, the beauty of a pergola depends overwhelmingly on the plants that clothe it. In the late 1800s, climbing roses, clematis, honeysuckle and wisteria gave eye-catching proof that they were as capable as grapevines of providing shade, while appealing to the eye and delighting the nostrils.

Tunnels, galleries and alleys, popular in England and America, are formed using a series of parallel arches over which, as on a pergola, vines or other climbers are encouraged to scramble. It is delightful in summer to pass from light to shade, from the heat to scent-laden coolness. Set at the entrance to a garden, the tunnel or alley can lead to a major feature; set further back, it offers a gentle transition between two distinct areas. The delicate woodwork carried out by medieval carpenters gave way to arches

COLLECTING TIP

You may find tunnels or parts of pergolas made of wrought iron in salvage yards or at antique dealers. They are usually in a shocking state and very expensive. But their sinuous charm is often worth the hours spent brushing off the rust. Another solution is to opt for reproductions — once covered in plants, they are indistinguishable from the real thing!

TOP
Pergola by J.-B. Papworth (1775–1847).

OPPOSITE
(top) Metal arches, in a deliberately random arrangement, span a short paved stairway. (bottom) This teak bench looks all the better for being framed by a romantic rose tunnel.

OVERLEAF
The path beside this large greenhouse is lined with greenery and roofed with vine arches; the effect is of a natural gallery.

created from wrought iron; today supports for tunnels are still made of these two materials.

An arbour is a light structure of wood, trellis, or from the nineteenth century, ironwork, surmounted by semicircular arches for plants to clamber over. Very popular in Mediterranean countries, because it provides shade without obstructing the passage of air and light, the arbour was a favourite spot for meditation with the Greeks and Romans, before becoming a lovers' trysting place and a venue for secret encounters. Square or round, classical or Palladian, in the Turkish or Japanese style, it has kept pace with prevailing fashions down the centuries.

OPPOSITE

(top) This pair of wooden pyramids were designed to support topiary; they are placed on wooden tubs in which the trees would have been planted.
(bottom) Roses twine up rustic poles driven into the ground.

TOPIARY SUPPORTS

Topiary, the art of clipping hedges and shrubs like box and yew into decorative forms, has existed since classical times and sometimes rigid supports were used to train the shapes. Today it is possible, using a shaped wire frame, to make plants grow into a range of different forms. Originally these frames were shaped like a cross or a crown and designed for florists to use as a base for preparing floral tributes offered at funerals. Today, animals such as birds, deer, sheep, rabbits, dogs and cats are among the most popular shapes for metal structures, though geometrical forms such as pyramids and obelisks still retain a following. Clipping a bush into shape can take five to ten years but, using these special frames, plants like ivy can be grown to cover them very quickly — or you can simply cover them with moss.

boundaries, gates and screens

Various kinds of material, including earth, wood, stone and metal, have been put to use at different times and places to mark off boundaries. In Egypt, Greece and Rome, wooden or trelliswork barriers were frequently used to enclose pleasure or vegetable gardens. In the Middle Ages, wood was the general rule, with chestnut, hazel, hornbeam and willow pressed into service to enclose monastic plots and control overflowing beds of ornamentals, aromatic and medicinal herbs, and plants to make dyes. Fencing and trellis also became an integral part of the highly architectural seventeenth-century garden. In the Romantic-style gardens of the 1700s, their purpose was less structural, but they were still ubiquitous. From Renaissance times, wrought iron was used alongside stone in Italian gardens, but it was in seventeenth- and eighteenth-century France that ironwork reached the pinnacle of its development. Gates and railings of great estates became virtual labyrinths of wrought iron, sometimes gilded into the bargain, as at Versailles. This passion for wrought iron reached England, thanks to the Huguenot Jean Tijou. The master of repoussé, he created magnificent gates and railings for the royal gardens at Hampton Court and laid the foundations of a highly influential English school of wrought iron work.

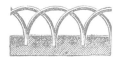

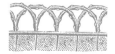

In the 1800s, industrialisation allowed the middle classes to enjoy the same sort of elaborate ironwork structures as the aristocracy, at less expense. Foundries issued mail order catalogues offering countless types of railings and gates that reproduced every possible historical style. It was not until the Art Nouveau movement arrived that designers found a new way of expressing themselves.

Today, taste has gone full circle, and the natural look is back in favour. We are more likely to find simple post-and-rail fences, Z-shaped gate structures and picket fences with shaped vertical laths, sometimes in mock Gothic style or with finials. Edgings can be made from continuous planking, a series of log rolls driven into the ground or lattice fastened to uprights. Rustic screens have incomparable charm. Made of willow, chestnut or hazel, they can be straightforward – simple arrangements of horizontal and vertical poles – or Gothic with withies or branches fastened to the cross-members and shaped into ogees, or in bundles, with the withies woven horizontally around log rolls. Framed panels of woven willow, bamboo, reed, or thatch, are equally effective in creating natural boundary effects.

TIP

Obviously wooden fence material, particularly the more rustic type, has a limited life-span. You should, therefore, consider treating it with a suitable plant-friendly preservative. To stop the bottoms of posts rotting in the ground, simply char them, either over the barbecue or in the fireplace. This will also stop wood boring insects from attacking them. To recognise genuinely old wrought-iron gates or railings, look for irregularities indicating the work was done by hand. The joints, in particular, are hammered, not riveted.

TOP
Three designs for wrought-iron arcading advertised in a catalogue from the Manufacture francaise d'armes et de cycles de Saint-Étienne dated 1914.

LEFT
A pair of wrought-iron gates under an iron arch open on to a narrow bridge.

OPPOSITE
(top) A wide metal pergola running from left to right is pierced by a pair of arches across a path set at right angles.
(bottom) Rustic fencing, with the tops of the palings attractively rounded.

OVERLEAF
Bordering a romantic pool, terracotta pots planted with tulips alternate, with dramatic effect, with female busts carved in stone.

BORDERS AND EDGINGS

Despite their modest dimensions, edgings are very important. They serve to hold back earth and gravel, surround a flowerbed, divide path from lawn – in short, add that final touch to the garden's appearance. Solid or in openwork forms like miniature grilles, they have evolved to suit changing tastes and occur in a variety of materials. Bricks can be set vertically, edgewise, angled in saw-tooth style, or cemented to make a low wall. You can use cobbles or granite setts, layers of pavers, a small wall of reconstituted stone, stone edging in the form of cable-twist, or frost-resistant cement blocks. Another possible material is terracotta; edgings are available as plain tiles or in more ornate styles with shaped tops and cable or swag decorations. The natural effect of wood is also very pleasing: a simple plank set into the ground and supported with pegs, a series of log rolls, twigs woven on to uprights or willow or bamboo bent into overlapping arcs will all make delightful borders. Another simple and solid material is ornamental wire, very much in vogue in the 1800s as scallop-shapes, semi-arcading with or without connecting ribs, or cast iron semi-circles imitating rustic branches. These are some of the easiest to install, as they come with spikes to push into the soil.

stone

wood

concrete and cement

cast iron

town and park benches

wrought iron

bamboo and rattan

wickerwork

Lloyd Loom

chestnut, hazel and rustic furniture

Garden furniture

chaises longues and deck chairs

small folding furniture

hammocks

parasols

stone

The stone seat, simple and solid, has existed since time immemorial. In classical times, garden furniture in the lands round the Mediterranean consisted of a few marble chairs and tables deftly disposed in shady spots. In contrast, in England in the Middle Ages, gardens were divided up into

small rooms following a grid pattern. Each square was filled with aromatic, medicinal and ornamental plants growing side by side, where visitors could rest on turf seats nestled in a cradle of sweet-smelling vegetation, screened by low brick walls. Illustrations of the period show that seats, made of stone or wooden tree trunks, also existed.

During the Renaissance, the gardens of Roman and Tuscan *palazzi* were filled with fountains, statues and vases recalling the splendours of the past with their processions of sphinxes, gods, mythical beasts and nymphs. Stone or marble seats sumptuously adorned with sculpted figures, flowers and foliage encouraged visitors to sit and admire this pagan marriage of nature with art. The Italian influence extended to gardens in France, Germany and to a lesser extent Holland. It was even felt in some regions of Spain with their mix of Arab and Andalusian culture. In the gardens of Seville and Cordoba stone benches and statuary rubbed shoulders with terracotta seats decorated with traditional Moorish tiles, whose vibrant colours added a deliciously fresh touch.

Following the Italian Renaissance, the French came to the fore as the garden designers of Europe with their conception of the garden as Man's domination of the landscape. Henceforth the model would be Versailles, with its grandiose yet harmoniously proportioned architecture designed to magnify the glory of the monarchy. In what is a masterly hymn to Apollo,

LEFT
Three simple benches, each consisting of a stone slab with low supports at either end – an ideal place to enjoy the pleasures of conversation.

OPPOSITE
The classic straight lines of this seat contrast with the arabesques of the cast-iron vase on the wall behind. The result is a perfect balance.

the Sun God, the ornamentation of the gardens sets off this domesticated rearrangement of Nature. The magnificently carved marble benches and seats scattered at strategic locations are part of this perfection.

The classic stone bench is composed of a lintel resting on two supports. Occasionally a back is added, extended by an upright at each end. The simplest is devoid of ornamentation, while more sophisticated developments, like those found in eighteenth-century chateaux, have decoration in the form of carved mouldings. Tables were similar to benches, made from a slab some 10–15 cm/4–6 in thick, mounted on supports.

The type of stone used varied according to the country, natural resources and climate. In Italy, the dominant trend was for marble, the finest quarries being those at Carrara and in the Valle d'Aosta. England had a preference

BELOW AND OPPOSITE
Examples of how to make good use of reclaimed objects. This elegant table consists of a marble top with a cast-iron grille serving as a central support. A similarly striking effect is produced by a stone slab resting on a pair of shapely jars.

COLLECTING TIP
Dating old stone benches is extremely difficult as they are not signed and bear no distinguishing mark. Copies made in the nineteenth and twentieth centuries, if exposed to the weather, acquire the same patina as the originals. It is best, therefore, to stick to a reasonable budget when buying. Stone is a noble material which harmonises well with trees and plants; it adds that touch of class to a garden which is hard to resist.

for Portland stone, a type of limestone from Dorset. In France, the popularity of marble was matched by that of granite from Brittany and the Tarn, sandstone from Alsace, the Vosges and around Fontainebleau as well as varieties of limestone found in Burgundy and the Seine valley.

From the 1700s, other materials, such as wood and cement, came into use, followed by iron a century later, but the popularity of stone has never been completely eclipsed. The stone bench may have evolved over the ages, but it still remains a timeless piece of garden furniture.

OVERLEAF
A table and a handful of chairs set in the shade. What more is needed to make the most of summer outside? (left) A set of chairs in the style of Hepplewhite. (right) A 1950s design made with wooden slats.

RECLAIMED STONE

By searching around salvage yards, you can pick up all sorts of
stone artefacts, and even pieces of sculpture, which you might
not instantly think of using to make garden furniture. An old
fireplace lintel laid across a couple of flat stones makes
a perfectly acceptable bench seat and so does a stone
garden roller. Why not turn the capital of a pillar into a seat or a
support for a table? With a bit of imagination, the possibilities
are endless.

OPPOSITE
This elegantly shaped bench has been covered with lichen over many years.

wood

ABOVE AND RIGHT
Two illustrations of chairs from the Magazine of Garden Gems published in 1802 by G. van Laur.

OPPOSITE
Whether made from simple rough-hewn planks fixed to supports shaped like branches, or an arrangement of logs nailed together, wooden seats weathered with time will not look out of place in any garden.

Until the Renaissance, the concept of furniture was strictly limited. The term principally denoted chests, buffets, benches and chairs. Tables were often no more than a plank set on trestles in a convenient place for mealtimes and subsequently removed. Pieces of furniture were made to measure by cabinet-makers in whatever hardwood was to hand – beech, chestnut, walnut and oak. Styles were uncomplicated, with seats mere variations on farmhouse originals. Most lacked backs; a few had simple backs in the form of a panel or rails supported on uprights, together with armrests.

Any idea of garden furniture was unheard of, even if the view was occasionally enhanced with a scattering of stone benches. People would simply bring out a table and chairs from the house when circumstances required it.

It was in the mid-1700s that purpose-built garden furniture began to be created. The grandeur of Versailles was succeeded by a more natural and poetic vision of the garden. Into these new landscaped areas were blended discreet and original seats made from the branches or trunks of yew, pear and other common local species. In England, even more than in France, this rustic style, as it came to be known, was a runaway success.

Increasingly gardens began to be filled with long tables accompanied by benches with backs formed of spaced, vertical slats, and provided with armrests. They were made to order in hardwoods and later painted to resist deterioration. Wood is not the ideal material for this sort of furniture,

OVERLEAF
An outdoor lifestyle definitely includes the art of placing a seat and a table in exactly the right spot. Here the teak furniture, set either end of the pool, has gradually acquired an attractive greyish patina.

as it does not withstand wet weather well. It needs to be kept under cover for half the year and, of course, it is heavy to move and bulky to store. Production remained at relatively low levels until the start of the twentieth century when new woods that were rot-resistant began to be imported from south-east Asia into Europe. Prime amongst these was teak, nicknamed 'iron wood' because nails hammered into it do not rust.

The importation of teak increased the production of garden furniture to an industrial scale. Solid, hard and pleasant to the touch, it could be made into simple and elegant shapes to harmonise with the artistic ethos of the period, such as the Arts and Crafts Movement in England or Art Deco in France. An outstanding example is the bench by the great architect of the inter-war years, Edwin Lutyens (1869–1944), which has become a design classic. After the 1930s, designs changed little, and the same models were turned out again and again until the 1980s when production diversified thanks to talented new designers.

BELOW AND OVERLEAF
Thanks to its weather-resistance and ease of maintenance, the teak seat has become a classic since the start of the twentieth century. The Arts and Crafts Movement and Art Deco inspired several designs which are still reproduced today.

OPPOSITE
Three variations on the Adirondack chair: a fairly classic version, a rustic adaptation and an original creation with a hint of Rietveld's 'Red and Blue' chair.

TIP
It is absolutely essential to protect wood from the weather and repaint it frequently, apart from certain rot-resistant exotic species.
To clean wooden furniture, brush it with soapy water, rinse and allow to dry.
If you want to repaint or re-varnish it, first brush on paint-stripper. When the paint begins to crinkle, remove it using a paint scraper. Sand down the surface. Fill any cracks or holes with an oil-based wood filler, then lightly sand before repainting. Alternatively, finish with a coat of clear or coloured varnish.
Teak should be cleaned with soapy water. When dry, it can be 'fed' by applying a coat of teak oil with a paintbrush. Allow to dry, then polish.
To maintain unpainted, resinous wood, first apply an undercoat of turpentine. Then give it a patina by applying warm linseed oil until the wood is saturated. Allow to partially dry and then remove any excess with a cloth. Leave to dry completely for several days and then polish.

COLLECTING TIP
Period garden benches and seats are hard to find, and when restored they frequently fetch very high prices. It is best to go for pieces in their original unrestored condition, and give yourself the pleasure of rejuvenating them. Before buying, check for damage to the feet, back and seat and look carefully at any repair work, which detracts from the value. If you're looking for a mass-produced item or an import from the early 1900s, be careful. Since the 1950s, factories have been turning out a constant stream of reproductions.

THE ADIRONDACK CHAIR

The name derives from an American mountain range in New York State, where its predecessor, the Westport chair, was invented at the start of the twentieth century. Made from an assembly of spaced wooden laths, the Adirondack has two special features: wide armrests, and a back that slopes at the ideal angle. It is nearly always painted – the farmhouses of Maine favour a matte reddish-brown, chestnut or green, while on the Atlantic coast they choose blue-grey or white. Its rustic and naïve appearance continues to delight Americans. It was also a hit in Europe, especially France, where it featured in a mail-order catalogue for some twenty years, and examples can be found in all corners of the globe. It is still manufactured in a number of workshops in the Adirondacks and can be bought by mail order. It returned to popular favour in Europe in the 1980s with the introduction of more sophisticated versions, notably in teak.

concrete and cement

TIP
Moulded cement or concrete furniture is largely unaffected by weather, though cement can suffer slight frost-damage. A large sheet of plastic will provide sufficient winter protection.
If the cement cracks, allowing water to penetrate, then the metal rods used to reinforce the concrete can rust, causing the piece to shatter.
The only cleaning required is a good wash now and again.

From the middle of the eighteenth century, the Versailles style, which had long dominated garden design, began to lose ground. Its formalism, provoked a fierce reaction and led to a desire to return to nature's former freedom. In England, a style was born which rediscovered nature through painting. It was called the landscaped garden; a dream-like vision, without strict boundaries, a garden that seemed, to all intents and purposes, completely natural. Garden furniture formed part of this vision. Allusions to the classical past were rejected in favour of more modest craft productions.

Towards the end of the century, in this same spirit of natural simplicity, a new means of making garden furniture from cement made its appearance in France. The raw material, a mixture of clay and lime, was moulded round a wire core by specialists, to imitate trunks and branches, and even included the texture of the bark and knots. This style, known as *rocaille* in France, re-emerged on a grand scale in the late 1900s, flourishing throughout Europe, especially in England, and extended to the United States. In the course of subsequent decades it underwent several changes in fortune, sometimes all the rage, at other times falling out of favour. Furniture made from cement was consigned to limbo between the 1950s and 1980, when a new generation of admirers arose particularly for those benches that graced public parks, spas and seaside resorts of the thirties. During the 1900s, alongside cement, another similar material came into prominence. It was concrete, which consisted of cement, sand and gravel or broken stone. It can be reinforced, like cement, by moulding it around an iron core. Heavy and durable, it was ideal for making furniture for use in urban public gardens, and it was used without restraint after the Second World War not only in public parks but also in the gardens of private individuals with a taste for the contemporary. Fine pieces from this period, many in a style derived from Art Deco, can still be found today.

COLLECTING TIP
Cement and concrete have the same advantages as stone. They both withstand rough weather and their weight should, in theory at least, act as a protection against theft.
Choose the spot for your table or seats carefully in advance, so that you won't need to reposition them.
There are several different models available, many of them reproductions, and prices vary. Eighteenth-century pieces are extremely rare and very expensive. Some items are unique, produced in the client's own garden by a craftsman specialising in rocaille work. The moulded versions were mass-produced. The three things to bear in mind are condition, quality and originality.

BOTTOM
The personal touch – the craftsman or customer has used his initials to form an integral part of the back of this bench.

RIGHT
Private individuals commissioned cement workers to produce unique pieces for every corner of the garden. As well as tables, benches and balustrades, they also created wells, flooring, bird tables and even dog kennels, as shown here.

The versatility of cement can fulfil almost any design demands. Here it is used to form branch-like supports for two semi-circular bench seats.

In the 1950s, these cement artifacts were adored by some and loathed by others. Today, their uncomplicated, period look attracts many collectors, perhaps because they recall the happier times that followed the end of the war.

Derived from Italian baroque, *rocaille* — a name coined in France — was born in the 1800s and lasted some four decades. A sharp break with classical tradition, it derived its inspiration from the artificial grottoes of the Renaissance with their fountains and nymphs. These in turn owed their origin to the grottoes of classical times. Mingling the rustic and the fantastic, the style was characterised by asymmetric and prolific decoration which included shells, snaking flower garlands, palms, winged dragons, etc. The style soon spread throughout Europe, especially in Germany, where it developed into rococo, and in England where it was called rustic. *Rocaille* artists often made seats in the form of shells, with sinuous lines and whimsical ornamentation; another trademark was shells and pebbles encrusted with cement.

TOP LEFT
Designs for garden structures which appeared in the 1902 edition of the Magazine of Garden Gems by G. van Laur.

TOP RIGHT
Eighteenth-century rocaille chair shaped like a scallop shell. It matches the wall decoration behind it.

ABOVE AND OPPOSITE
In the 1940s and 50s many gardens, both private and public, installed fixed seats which needed no maintenance. These benches, made from green mosaic set in cement, co-ordinate with the material and motifs used in the paving.

cast iron

COLLECTING TIP

Cast iron is reasonably weather proof but it can shatter, which explains the scarcity of original pieces. Another reason is that old designs were thrown away and replaced by others in more contemporary taste. Always check there are no makeshift repairs that may conceal serious damage. The work of the art foundries nearly always bears the foundry signature.

From the 1850s, increased urbanisation gave rise to a powerful nostalgia for nature in Europe's major towns and spas. In response, public gardens and squares were laid out so that locals and visitors taking the cure could stroll down long promenades or sit round the bandstands and listen to music. As a result, there arose a need for specifically open-air furniture, and this was fulfilled by cast iron, a new material that had arrived on the scene.

Cast iron is an alloy of carbon and iron created by fusion. Iron had been employed for the making of household utensils since the fifteenth century, but its usefulness only really took off as new metallurgical processes were developed, particularly the invention of a casting process. The resulting material was easy to work, cheap, and could be mass-produced, all of which made it ideal for garden furniture. It was weather-resistant, which allowed objects to remain outside all year, and its solidity and weight ensured it was quite stable. Painted in white, black or green, benches, chairs and tables joined pairs of gates and lamp posts in public gardens. This was a stylistically eclectic age, rich in technical progress and yet deeply imbued with ideas from the past. Early cast-iron furniture designs were inspired by gothic or classical styles and even a mixture of the two. Towards the middle of the century, designs gained in originality, becoming lighter and incorporating animals and plants. Ferns, vines, laurel, serpents and squirrels began to be incorporated into the backs of benches and chairs. In France, a number of foundries turned out this sort of furniture and in England, the Coalbrookdale and Britannia foundries exported throughout Europe, and examples of their work could be found in the palaces of Istanbul and India.

TOP AND OPPOSITE

Nineteenth-century cast-iron seats. (opposite page) retro styling recalling the 1700s; (top left) chair with classic fern motif; (centre) English Coalbrookdale bench in stitch pattern; (right) lightweight bench with vine leaf decoration in the back.

ABOVE

Two cast-iron chairs from the Magazine of Garden Gems published in 1902 by G. van Laur.

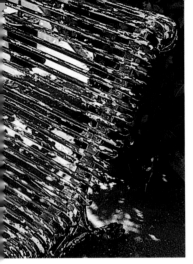

town and park benches

TIP

To renovate an old bench, use paint stripper on the metal parts, then sand down to remove final traces of rust or paint. Rub down the wood with medium glasspaper and fill any cracks with an oil-based wood filler. Finally, repaint the bench using specialised oil-based wood and metal paints. Alternatively, the wood can be varnished.

TOP

Many public parks contain this style of metal bench that has become a design classic.

BOTTOM

Cast-iron frame designs for garden benches from the 1887 foundry catalogue of Hauts-Fourneaux, Fonderies et Ateliers de Construction de Tusey (Meuse)

In the nineteenth century, the opening up of squares and tree-lined avenues in the cities, and the birth of a modern public transport system with the building of surface and underground stations, created the need for what we now call urban furniture. This included public seating for people waiting for trains and trams, which meant, more often than not, benches made from cast iron and wood. Frames made from cast iron – a solid, cheap material capable of being mass-produced – were the ideal base for attaching wide oak slats to form seats and seat backs. Oak is hard and solid and once painted offers resistance to the weather. Benches were made in single or double versions, the latter set back to back with the same back piece serving both benches. A second design used narrow rounded slats of beech, pine, fir or even metal, which were set close together in a sinuous curve over an iron frame. Somewhat more ergonomic, it had the advantage of not leaving any large gaps.

These benches were usually about 2 m/6 ft long. They were fixed in place with a bolt into a base buried in the ground, but could be moved if the need arose. In the early 1900s, the same iron-and-wood designs were reduced in length and from the 1950s, they were frequently replaced by designs in concrete or synthetic materials. Nonetheless, their attractive shapes have not completely vanished from towns and versions are still produced today.

COLLECTING TIP

Some benches still bear the traces of having been bolted to foundations, which is a good sign of authenticity. You are more likely to find examples with wide, oak slats, which last longer, than those with narrow curving slats made of less durable woods. Such is their popularity that these designs are still produced today, though contemporary versions tend to be lighter and smaller. If you just find the metal frame you can easily make up the wooden seat and back yourself.

OPPOSITE

A public bench which has taken on a new lease of life in someone's garden.

OVERLEAF

Perfect partnerships of wood and iron.

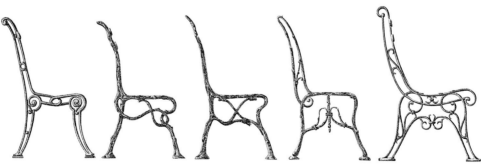

wrought iron

The creation of public parks went hand in hand with the increase in privately owned gardens. When the upper middle classes began to take holidays in luxurious country houses tucked away on grand estates, there was no longer any question of them making do with furniture in wood or stone. While cast iron found its place in public areas, wrought iron invaded private gardens. It was resistant to the weather, solid yet light, which meant it could be moved around easily and taken indoors over winter, if necessary.

Until the mid-nineteenth century, this type of furniture was made by independent craftsmen. Now numerous small ironwork forges began to experiment with mass production. In England, France and Germany they flooded the home markets and exported abroad using a system of mail-order catalogues. Both detailed and well presented, they offered an incredible range of furniture with every conceivable variation.

In France the Napoleon III style, then in vogue for interiors, also found expression in garden furniture. Its characteristic was exuberant ornamentation inspired by the preceding centuries and, in particular, *rocaille*. The frames used were fairly uniform, but chair backs, seats and foot rests as well as the tops of tables occurred in a multiplicity of shapes and sizes. Designs included wide straps intersecting in lozenge shapes, fine network patterns and pierced metal sheets imitating basketwork or lace. Manufacturers made it a matter of honour to extend their imagination and skill. One company created sprung seats and chair backs with flexible, curving slats, another produced an interesting range of rocking-chairs and there were even chairs whose feet ended in flat claws that would not sink into the earth. Designs continued to be influenced by fashion and, towards the end of the century, Art Nouveau, which took its inspiration from nature, imposed a more fluid style with elegant and sinuous lines; while Art Deco, which followed, was dominated by more geometric shapes with stylised ornament.

TIP
Check for rust regularly and take action immediately it appears by rubbing with steel wool. To avoid deterioration, repaint iron furniture regularly. Once the old paint has been stripped off, apply a coat of anti-rust paint and finish with another of an oil-based metal paint. Some oil-based paints have anti-rust properties.

OPPOSITE
(top) Two splendid old bench-style seats made from a combination of wrought iron and wood. The scrolled armrests are more aesthetic than practical.
(bottom left) A pedestal table in wrought iron with a hole for a parasol – a style which is still in fashion today.
(bottom right) This wrought-iron chair with wide, well-spaced slats is an object lesson in harmony and balance.

TOP AND BELOW
Catalogue designs from Les Besoins de la vie *from 1887, advertising a bench with canopy and a chair, both with sprung metal slats.*

COLLECTING TIP

Period wrought iron was made using very pure metal, and rusts very little in comparison with modern versions. Seats identical to those produced in the nineteenth century are still made today, which makes dating extremely risky.
A couple of tips to look out for – old pieces are heavier and are normally riveted, whereas reproductions are welded and the workmanship is less perfect.
Some outlets have begun selling old pieces that have been sanded down and lacquered, revealing their original beauty. But this specialist work comes at a price. Period frames can also be restored with new cane work and wooden slats. Items originating from some of the art foundries are numbered and marked on the base.

RIGHT

A simple combination of wooden laths and an iron frame, these light folding chairs were mass-produced in all sorts of variations for parks and public gardens. They are part of the cultural memory for many people.

OPPOSITE

Elegant, with fine, curving lines, these seats have a presence that is distinct but discreet.

FRENCH CHAISES DE SQUARE

In France, in the past, folding chairs were hired out for a few centimes in public parks. They had an iron frame and wooden slatted seats and were produced in huge numbers. They are still easy to find today at second-hand markets, sometimes sold unrestored in their original condition. Many collectors prefer them like this.

bamboo and rattan

COLLECTING TIP

Prices of old rattan and bamboo furniture vary according to quality, condition and rarity. Nineteenth-century work is incredibly rare and practically no pieces exist. The newer models, plain and without signature, remain affordable. Some seats have the manufacturer's name on an oval plaque, which adds to their value.

TOP AND BOTTOM

Designs from the Manufrance catalogue issued in the early twentieth century.

OPPOSITE

Rattan is very supple and the weave can be tight or loose. It can be left plain and varnished or coloured, and it is sometimes combined with other materials like wicker and bamboo.

Rattan is derived from a species of climbing palm that can grow to 300 m/1,000 ft. It is a native of south-east Asia, particularly India and Malaya. In its natural condition it is the colour of honey – though with some variation in shades – but it can be dyed or painted. Different parts of the plant are used in making furniture: the outer bark, the whole cane and the pith at the centre of the cane. Furniture frames are constructed of the whole canes, which are bent to shape using steam heat. They are now ready to be assembled and reinforced. The fine inner pith of the canes is used to make the weave of the seat, arms and back. For cane seating, the outer bark is sliced into thin strips. Once the back, seat and frame are assembled, all that remains is to bind the parts that need reinforcing.

Bamboo resembles rattan, but its stems are hollow and lack pith. Light and supple, yet durable, it has regular ridges, which give it its aesthetic character. Bamboo lends itself well to making rattan chair carcasses and the stems can also be split and used to make tabletops.

In 1851, many of the traditional skills of Chinese craftsman were displayed at the Great Exhibition in London. This included cane furniture and it sent Western visitors and collectors into transports of delight. In fact, the Dutch had imported rattan a century earlier for use in the seats and backs of chairs. From the 1800s, ready-made rattan and bamboo

TIP

If rattan begins to split, feed it once or twice a year with linseed oil or a little silicon-free beeswax.
If a piece of furniture has gone out of shape or the legs are broken, contact a specialist repairer.
To mend a broken strand, bend it back into shape or cut it off neatly and tie it in with strong thread or a thin strip of leather.
Rattan likes a slightly damp atmosphere; if it creaks excessively, it is too dry. Freshen it up now and again by spraying it with water and leave it to dry in the shade.
To bleach, use warm water to which has been added five tablespoons of hydrogen peroxide or lemon juice to 1 litre/1¾ pints. Brush on and leave to dry in an airy place out of the sun.

Two designs for beach seats, in wickerwork and rattan, from an early twentieth-century catalogue produced by Manufacture des Armes et Cycles de Saint-Étienne.

Afternoon in the Garden *by Alain Bazard, c. 1944.*

furniture began to be imported from China and Manila. Extremely light and finely crafted, they combined the charm of natural material with the novelty of the exotic. Above all, they were just as useful outside as indoors. Firms rushed to stock them, while craftsmen copied and modified the designs. In the twentieth century catalogues began offering dozens of designs whose forms, at first heavily inspired by the Orient, evolved swiftly into a more European style. The weave could be tight, loose, or openwork; the material might be all one colour, or with decorative stripes or geo-metric shapes in red, blue, turquoise, green or black. Production was on a huge scale and customers ranged from private individuals to hotel and steamship companies. The range extended to sofas, dining tables, occasional tables, worktables, chairs, armchairs, stools and chaises-longues.

Demand waned between the wars, but resumed even more strongly in the 1950s. Today, it is plastic reproductions that are flooding the market.

An astonishing range of styles and weaves from a colour catalogue of Maxime Clair et ses fils, *1911.*

wickerwork

Wicker furniture is made from a small, moisture-loving willow at home on riverbanks and low-lying areas prone to flooding. The willow wands are planted in rows and harvesting begins with the first frosts and continues until February. The leaves are pruned and the rods are tied into bundles, to be soaked in shallow water or put into a boiler until the bark softens and can be stripped off. Willow that has been soaked leaves wands of a fine, creamy-white colour; boiled willow is a golden brown. Bundled up again, they are kept in a dry, shady place until needed, and worked either whole or split into strips.

For hundreds of years basket makers had turned out a large number of artefacts, yet furniture still remained something of an afterthought. But the importation of rattan furniture from China in the late 1800s meant things changed quickly and soon, in the catalogues of the early 1900s, the number of rattan chairs was equalled by wicker versions. Willow was local and available, aesthetally pleasing and the skills to work with it already existed, passed down for centuries from generation to generation.

Willow can be woven in many different ways and it may be left in its natural state, varnished, or given a coloured lacquer. A range of designs gradually saw the light of day including loungers, chairs and sofas with deep-buttoned cushions, tables, chaises longues and chairs with seat, back and armrests padded with cretonne upholstery. More unusual designs included individual or two-person beach chairs with high sides and a roof, made with a thick weave to give protection against the wind, and armchairs with dramatic backs and wings that enveloped the sitter. Sometimes willow and rattan were used together, with the framework in the former and the seat and back – or the top in the case of a table – made from the finer pithy inner core of rattan.

Like rattan, willow would fall out of favour, though a few original creations drew interest in the 1950s.

COLLECTING TIP
Check the condition of any chair you purchase. It should be stable, and have retained its shape. Look out for broken strands and check that it does not creak too much. For it to be a bargain you need to be able to restore it yourself.

TIP

To clean wickerwork, use trisodium phosphate diluted in water. Rinse thoroughly and leave to dry outside, out of the sun.
Over time willow can acquire a rather unattractive greyish coloration. To return it to its original paler tint, dilute a tablespoon of bleach in 1 litre/1¾ pints of water. Scrub vigorously with a brush (not one with wire bristles), rinse and leave to dry.

RIGHT AND BELOW
A chair and a bench – half-furniture, half-shrub – formed from living willow. Green willow wands are planted in the ground and then woven together. Watered regularly in the normal way, they sprout a covering of tender green foliage.

LIVING WILLOW

The delightful tradition of working with living willow is being revived in today's gardens. It is principally used for fences and screens, but it can equally well make a seat back or a garden bench. Simply dig out a trench about 30 cm/12 in deep around the seat and plant the rods, either in a straight line, or weave them together to make the shape of the back. Water them thoroughly and often and they will resume growth and sprout attractive foliage.

Lloyd Loom

In 1917, the American industrialist Marshall B. Lloyd — who was also responsible for a couple of hundred other inventions such as a fishing rod, a wire-fibre doormat and a machine for making steel pipes — came up with a new process for creating wickerwork. The material he used was not his own invention — a twisted fibre made of kraft paper and glue — but he improved it by reinforcing it with steel wire. His idea was to produce a quality weave without the need to employ specialist labour. Traditionally, the craftsman first creates a framework and then weaves the trim around it. Lloyd's method was to separate the two parts of the task, weaving the trim in sheets and then nailing it to the structure. The weaving was done using large spools, avoiding the need to join separate lengths of fibre, always a weakness with materials like rattan and willow. Thanks to this new method of working and the many advantages of the material itself, Lloyd Loom was a great success. The resulting products were smooth to the touch, the strands didn't snag clothing; they were resistant to sun or rain, and aged well without sagging, splitting or losing their shape.

At first, Lloyd applied his technique solely to the manufacture of children's prams and baby carriages. It rapidly became a hit. In 1922, he extended it to furniture, flooding the American market. In 1928, his company's catalogue was advertising over 80 designs. Production began to run out of steam from 1933, and after the war diminished still further until it ceased in the sixties.

The story of Lloyd Loom would have remained an entirely American affair had not the English industrialist, William Lusty, whose imagination was fired by the new product, obtained the rights for Great Britain in 1921. After a hesitant start, Lusty was immensely successful, and his factory became as productive as Lloyd's, supplying middle-class homes and luxury hotels alike. His 1933 catalogue included more than 400 designs, among which were sofas, rockers, occasional tables, coffee tables, fire screens, jardinières, nursery furniture, hat stands, desks, chests and laundry baskets. During the Second World War, the factory was completely destroyed by an air raid. Lusty tried to start again from scratch, but this time his luck ran out, production tailed off and the works closed in 1968.

COLLECTING TIP

Lloyd Loom items are once again available, but from different companies, including the American firm Lloyd-Flanders. Period pieces, particularly those made by Lusty, have a label with the date of manufacture, which is best deciphered by an expert. To distinguish the genuine article from copies, check for the presence of metal wires inside the fibres, using a magnet if necessary. A Lloyd Loom is worth more in its original colour, less if it has been repainted. Prices depend on the condition of the original paint, lack of damage, rarity and demand — the most sought-after articles are coffee tables, children's furniture and large sofas.

TIP

To clean Lloyd Loom, first vacuum off the dust. Then protect the manufacturer's label by sticking a piece of plastic over it before washing it down with a soft brush and soapy water. Leave to dry in the open air or the sun. In general, you should not repaint Lloyd Loom. If you have to, use an aerosol and spray as lightly as possible so as not to block the spaces between the weave.

TOP LEFT

Every article leaving the Lloyd Loom factory carried a label. They varied in type, allowing for fairly precise dating.

OPPOSITE

Lloyd Loom, with its kraft paper fibres reinforced by steel wires, revolutionised the world of lightweight furniture. This armchair, a real classic, was originally intended for the conservatory or garden, but since the 1930s they made their way into countless English drawing-rooms and bedrooms.

chestnut, hazel and rustic furniture

The chestnut tree was originally a native of Asia Minor, and well known to the Greeks and Romans. As the latter extended their conquest of Europe, they encouraged the growing of this useful tree. Exploited both for its fruits and its wood, chestnut can be made into fences, trellis, hoops for barrels and casks, tool handles, general woodwork articles and also simple, rustic furniture, the latter particularly in France.

Few woods are as straightforward as chestnut. It is fast growing, with no special requirements; it is very light, sheds water, and – an added bonus – splits easily and is simple to work. Though chestnut trees can reach 30 m/100 ft in height, it is more profitable to coppice them. A similar technique is used with hazel. The trunk of the tree is cut, and the tree puts out several new stems from the stump, and as these are regularly harvested, new stems grow.

The harvest takes place from October to March, when the poles are cut, the side growth stripped away and they are sawn to the size required. The logs are used as uprights for fencing and plant stakes and the thinner lengths for furniture making. Before they are bundled according to size, the bark may be removed.

For furniture, not only the thinner lengths but also the split branches – once used to make barrel hoops – are important. Pieces that have retained their bark possess an attractive brown colour with a light tinge of grey.

The woodworker removes the knots with a plane made from a sharp blade with a handle at each end. The whitish mark left by the cut contrasts with the brown bark and lends the furniture a natural appearance. The lengths to be used are then shaped over a wooden trestle after being softened in boiling water. The split branches are used to form the circular seats of traditional armchairs and fine, criss-cross strips can be fixed to a curved frame to make flexible chair backs.

Chestnut furniture is both rustic and unpretentious. For centuries, these articles were made by farmers and agricultural workers for purely domestic use. In the 1950s in France, gypsies took over the manufacture of these articles, hawking their wares around the countryside. These basic, natural-looking pieces, lovingly put together, bring back a flood of memories and today sophisticated reproductions are appearing in limited editions.

Chestnut was also used on a large scale in the late nineteenth and early twentieth centuries to make frames for garden seats. Cheap and solid, once the bark is removed it forms an ideal frame for woven rattan or willow.

ABOVE
The rustic look of this jardinière conceals the technical skill needed to make it.

CENTRE
Armchair of bent hazel wood – a classic of its type.

ABOVE
Miniature cupboard fashioned from bark and small branches.

TOP

Driftwood, stripped of its bark and polished by the water, can make highly imaginative features. The creator of this ingenious seat has sought out longer branches and used their curves in the design.

RIGHT

The addition of a frieze of small half-rolls under the top lends this table an added charm.

COLLECTING TIP

The chestnut furniture you come across will not be more than a few decades old. But even pieces made today have all the appeal of natural materials and the unassuming naiveté of popular art.

You may also turn up some real curiosities, one-off, rugged homemade pieces made from logs. Their price depends on their originality, workmanship and condition. Mass-produced items are starting to become rare. Ignore any in poor condition, as major restoration is difficult.

chaises longues and deck chairs

The ancestor of the chaise longue belonged to the age of Louis XV. It was a deep, padded chair, with an extension for the sitter's legs. If a chaise longue was all in one piece, it was known as a *duchesse*, if in two or three sections, a *duchesse brisée*. In the same spirit as daybeds and ottomans, the chaise longue allowed women, for whom they were exclusively manufactured, to adopt a languid, semi-reclining pose.

In the 1800s, manufacturers had the idea of making similar chairs for outdoor use. All that was needed was to remove the upholstery, leaving the wood bare, and to connect the three sections with hinges to make them easily portable. Initially manufactured in beech or ash, as a one-off piece or in short runs, it went into mass production with the arrival of imported teak at the end of the nineteenth century.

At about the same time wickerwork models appeared and their lightness and the beauty and suppleness of the weave immediately made them popular. Rattan recliners in styles inspired by the Far East were turned out by the thousand, both to order and mass-produced. The chairs were either in one piece or could be folded into three parts; the angle of the back was adjustable on some versions, and there might be a headrest and padded arms. They could be covered with canvas, and some came with a rectangular canvas sunshade. The weave and the colours used were as varied as those of modern garden sets.

TIP

If some parts of a piece are in poor condition, they can often be repaired or replaced by a specialist. Metal hinges can also be easily renewed. Chairs made of beech or other European species require waxing two or three times a year. Teak should be brushed with linseed or teak oil or melted, silicon-free beeswax. Put a few drops of oil on the metal hinges.

STEAMER CHAIRS AND DECK CHAIRS

At the end of the nineteenth and beginning of the twentieth century, the fashion for taking ocean cruises reached its height. As always, demand created supply. Passengers liked to take the air on deck, so they were provided with loungers complete with small footrests. Originally used on steamships they came to be known as steamer chairs and were durable, comfortable, and easy to move around. At first they were made entirely of wood, but became lighter and less cumbersome thanks to the racked legs still in use today and the combination first of ash — or bamboo — with cane work. Deck chair is a term that has now come to refer to the folding wood and canvas chair popular on beaches and in parks and gardens.

small folding furniture

In the latter half of the nineteenth century, people spent more of their leisure time out of doors. There was an increased interest in sport, and a new activity was born – camping. The result was a challenge to furniture-makers' imaginations. To suit the weekend painter, angler or hunter, they created lightweight folding seats which could be carried anywhere.

The simplest versions were folding stools made of varnished wooden slats fixed to a lightweight metal frame; alternatively the whole stool might be made of metal. Both types folded completely flat. A more sophisticated type followed the same pattern but boasted a cane seat. Some could even be adapted for use on a slope.

The hunter's version, well crafted and rather dashing, was a three-legged affair in plain varnished wood, over which was stretched a piece of grained leather, or canvas with leather reinforcements at the corners, to form the seat. Another innovation aimed at the sportsman was the shooting-stick, in varnished wood and metal.

The folding beach stool allowed the occupant to relax in style. It was made of varnished or painted ash, sometimes carved to imitate bamboo, and had a seat of brightly striped canvas. In the same style, and not much heavier, was the folding chair. It was constructed identically to the stool, but the ash frame included a back. Both the back and seat were made from striped canvas, sometimes in two sections. Then came a more luxurious version – the armchair. It was usually a bamboo structure with a caned seat and a back of tapestry-style woven canvas, from which the fabric armrests were also made.

Another variant of the canvas armchair is what today is called a director's chair. The frame was of hand-turned wood and the back and seat made from canvas bands, often with horizontal stripes. Most of the above-mentioned items came in three sizes, for men, women and children.

BOTTOM

A series of folding canvas chairs, in ash and bamboo, from the Maxime Clair et ses fils *1911 catalogue.*

OPPOSITE

Artists, hunters, anglers and ramblers with a penchant for contemplation would not dream of setting out without their folding stool.

COLLECTING TIP

Small wooden stools can be picked up fairly cheaply. These delightful items are generally restored and the canvas is likely to be a modern replacement.

Even the famous house of Thonet surrendered to the fashion for folding seats with this little chair – a far cry from their usual lines.

hammocks

In the late 1800s, the increase in open-air activities and the steady rise in the popularity of camping gave rise to new concepts of outdoor living. This period saw the introduction of the hammock, the hanging bed originally from South America and long in use on board sailing ships. Woven from cream or multicoloured cotton, some have beech spreaders at each end to keep the fabric spaced out. They are very portable as they simply roll up and pack away in a small carrying bag.

The modern hammock has come a long way since the original versions used by our ancestors. For gardens or campsites where there are no trees, you can buy lightweight, collapsible hammock stands. Other forms of suspended seating were also developed, including hanging chairs woven from willow and swing seats with integral sunshades. All sizes of people were catered for, from babies to adults, and many of these articles had their own foldaway stands.

OPPOSITE
The Mexican way – two hammocks made of cotton, with broad fringes, slung between two trees. A perfect reminder of the joys of outdoor living and lazy holidays spent doing nothing!

BOTTOM
Three hammocks from a French catalogue, Manufacture des Armes et Cycles de Saint-Étienne.

RIGHT
From a plain length of material to intricately knotted and crocheted designs, the hammock is just as at home on a veranda or balcony as in the garden.

TOP

October, by K. Ferenczy (1862–1917).

OPPOSITE

(top) The large, plain cotton parasol has become a classic. Yet manufacturers in the early 1900s showed much more ingenuity and imagination than their modern counterparts, as can be seen from the designs from mail order catalogues given below. (bottom) English designs for seats with parasols dating from the nineteenth century.

parasols

At a time when a tanned complexion was considered socially unacceptable, parasols and sunshades were indispensable for anyone wanting to enjoy the beach or garden without catching the direct rays of the sun. Parasols were usually made in plain or striped cloth and often sported a big fringe. They were round or pagoda-shaped. Some could be adapted for use with garden chairs by means of a metal claw that attached to the back of the seat. Ironwork tables were made with a central hole to take the handle of a large parasol.

Sunshades were also adapted for benches. Some had a roof structure made from upright and horizontal metal bars covered with canvas to provide shade. Many chairs, folding armchairs and swing chairs also boasted similar rigid rectangular sunshade supports. Occasionally furniture even came with matching side curtains to give complete all round protection!

COLLECTING TIP
Obviously, period hammocks and sunshades will not have survived a century of wear and tear. At best, you'll have to make do with one of those rather kitsch versions from the 1950s.

TIP
To clean the material of a sunshade, unfold it completely and brush vigorously with soapy water. Leave to dry thoroughly before refolding.

lamps and lanterns

garden games

aviaries and cages

nesting boxes, birdbaths and feeders

scarecrows and bird-scarers

basketry

Accessories

tools

cloches and greenhouses

watering cans

wheelbarrows, carts and trolleys

lamps and lanterns

COLLECTING TIP
All sorts of cheap, attractive lanterns can be found in second-hand shops but, unfortunately, most have lost their glass. If you are looking for a genuine antique be careful of fake imports from the Far East; the market is swarming with them. They will lack that telltale irregularity, spot of rust or interesting patina – though look alikes are just as decorative as the originals. Old ship's lanterns, whether made from old and rusty sheet iron or superb specimens in gleaming brass, look great in the garden with a candle inside. Copper or ironwork reproductions of old gas and oil lamps are very effective placed either side of a doorway.

The oil lamp, in use since Roman times, was the main source of light in country districts until the early 1930s. These lamps had a metal stem so they could be hung against a wall or from a beam. They were made of earthenware, brass, bronze or copper and used oil obtained from whatever was available locally. Oil was also used in lanterns, which were essentially metal boxes made from bronze and later painted ironwork or sheet iron. Early lanterns had translucent walls of oilpaper or horn to protect the flame, and these were replaced by glass when it became common. Grander versions were used to light the entrance halls and stairways of large country houses.

In the nineteenth century, candle lanterns made of iron and glass were generally available. The glass panels, which prevented the flame blowing out in the wind, were protected against knocks by a frame of wire shaped in a Y or a cross, and there was a chimney to increase the up draught. The candles of poorer country folk were made from tallow, beeswax being reserved for the gentry and the clergy. The discovery of stearic acid by Chevreul (1786–1889) led to the candle as we know it today and its cheapness and mass production led to the greater use of candles in chandeliers, lanterns and storm lanterns.

About 1870, lighting was greatly improved by the invention of the paraffin lamp. This consisted of a reservoir for the paraffin and a wick that burned through capillary action; the wick passed through a chamber pierced with air holes to assist combustion. The petrol lamp worked on the same principles, but without the need for an additional air supply.

Another important advance, in the late 1800s, was the carbide or acetylene lamp. Calcium carbide was contained in one reservoir, water in the other. When the two were brought into contact, acetylene gas was produced, and this was fed to an aperture where it could be ignited. It was an ingenious invention, certainly, but it had a drawback – the smell was

BOTTOM
Examples of old Japanese lanterns which were much sought-after, especially in England, in the early 1800s.

OPPOSITE
A small iron-and-glass lantern which is ideal for the garden. Hang several of these from a tree and use candles or electric bulbs as a light source.

OVERLEAF
Metal lamp holders, period street-lamps, lanterns or old glass jars with candles in them – they all look good in the garden and create that special night-time atmosphere.

obnoxious. Hence acetylene lamps tended to be mainly used out of doors. To find their way about in the dark, country folk, mountaineers and early campers used galvanised iron storm lanterns with protective metal surrounds. Lanterns made of brass, iron and glass were carried on the offside of horse-drawn vehicles; they also served as hand held lamps for the drivers. Bicycles were successively equipped with lamps lit by oil, candles, paraffin and acetylene. The same fuels supplied the copper and nickel headlamps of motorcars and early enamelled sheet iron lorry lamps. As for street lighting, this was first introduced to towns in Europe in the late seventeenth century. The grim use to which they were put during the French Revolution is well known and the phrase *les aristocrates à la lanterne* has passed into the French language. Street lamps, mounted on walls and, slightly later, freestanding, were powered by a variety of means – resin, wax, rapeseed oil, animal fat, and finally gas and electricity. So robust were these that they still linger on today in many a street.

In England, Victorian gardens were lit by gas lamps set on forged or cast iron standards and were the last word in contemporary fashion. In the early 1900s, hanging garden lamps made of nickelled copper were popular, with the gas mantle, in its metal mount, enclosed by a protective globe.

garden games

Pleasure gardens were first created in England in the eighteenth century, and they soon spread through Europe, developing the taste for outdoor games and activities. Some gardens were magnificently equipped, such as those at the French chateau at Rambouillet, which were furnished with toboggans, swings and a roller coaster – all for adults. The majority of the more modest gardens boasted, at the least, swings, bowling greens and archery butts.

It is amazing how many kinds of garden game were current in the late nineteenth and early twentieth centuries. Some like *spirobole*, an early version of tetherball, have disappeared, others still exist today, games like diabolo, boomerangs, stilts and cup-and-ball, but are mainly played by children. A few games like badminton and croquet are still played in large gardens but are losing popularity.

In France, for centuries, the favourite outdoor games were skittles and boules. Skittles is seen far less now, but boules is as popular as ever. The rules vary according to region and in 1910 a variation called pétanque was invented, which is played over a shorter distance.

Boules have evolved over time. Originally, the balls were made of stone, but in the 1800s its place was taken by wood, usually elm, or better still, box, both species known for their robustness. To prevent them wearing out too rapidly, boules were studded with nails arranged side by side or overlapping in scales. Some of them are set in attractive patterns of iron, brass and copper, others are more mundane; big round nails for playing in the street, chic square nails reserved mainly for ladies, heavy square heads, convex nails, or stainless steel nails – the variations are endless.

Skittles originated in Egypt, reaching Europe in about the 1500s. Early skittles were conical in shape, and a stick was used as the projectile. In the seventeenth century, the stick was replaced by a large wooden ball and

TIP
To restore the shine to a fine set of nailed boules, rub with glasspaper and then polish briskly with a cloth.

OPPOSITE TOP
Good, old-fashioned wooden skittles – for centuries this was one of the most popular garden games among young and old alike.

OPPOSITE BOTTOM
Nailed boules may have gone out of fashion to play with, yet they remain sought-after by collectors, who consider them highly attractive.

then, in some areas, by a ball with a hole for the thumb and a larger slit for the other fingers. To begin with there were eight elm-wood skittles – said to be one for each of the deadly sins plus one for the Devil – arranged in three ranks to form a triangle. The game developed in the late 1800s into tenpin bowling.

Other games of skill that were in vogue in the early 1900s included quoits which involves throwing rings on to a peg or a target set on a wall, clock golf where the numbers are set in a large circular clock face round a central hole and, in some formal gardens, large-scale version of chess or draughts. In France a game called *jeu de tonneau* or frog table was popular. The table was a sloping oak board, featuring an open-mouthed frog, hoops, and holes, mounted on a barrel or stand. Players tossed lead discs on to the board, trying to make them land in the numbered holes.

BOTTOM
Two games of tonneau *(frog table) advertised in the* Manufacture francaise d'Armes et de Cycles de Saint-Étienne *catalogue of 1913.*

OPPOSITE
Garden games were immensely popular in the early 1900s, particularly croquet (top), badminton and frog table (below).

COLLECTING TIP
Croquet sets found today usually consist of six to eight mallets and balls, a set of metal hoops and marker, complete with storage box. Old badminton rackets have gut strings on an ash frame. To complete the set you need a shuttlecock with white feathers and a net some 6 m/20 ft long mounted on posts.
It's not hard to find nailed boules in France as they resist any amount of wear. Look out for old garden games like tonneau *and* skittles. *As well as being interesting and attractive, there's every chance that a small amount of restoration will see them fit for use again.*

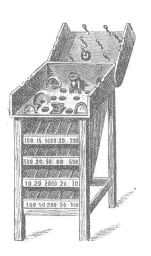

Le Jeu de Tonneau

aviaries and cages

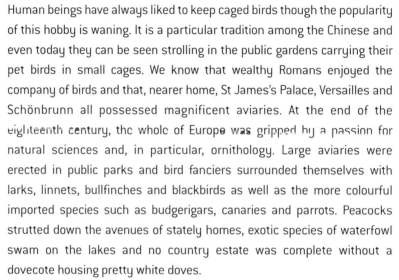

Human beings have always liked to keep caged birds though the popularity of this hobby is waning. It is a particular tradition among the Chinese and even today they can be seen strolling in the public gardens carrying their pet birds in small cages. We know that wealthy Romans enjoyed the company of birds and that, nearer home, St James's Palace, Versailles and Schönbrunn all possessed magnificent aviaries. At the end of the eighteenth century, the whole of Europe was gripped by a passion for natural sciences and, in particular, ornithology. Large aviaries were erected in public parks and bird fanciers surrounded themselves with larks, linnets, bullfinches and blackbirds as well as the more colourful imported species such as budgerigars, canaries and parrots. Peacocks strutted down the avenues of stately homes, exotic species of waterfowl swam on the lakes and no country estate was complete without a dovecote housing pretty white doves.

Birdcages, from the smallest to the grandest aviary, served as pretext to indulge in fantasies of design. Rustic cages were usually small – for a maximum of two birds – and made of natural materials like chestnut, bamboo, willow or a mixture of wire and wood. Their homemade, unpretentious qualities lend them a special charm. More refined were cages made from costly woods like mahogany, with the sides incorporating, in the 1800s, galvanised wire or fine wickerwork, and a century later, brass. These versions were tall, often divided into two storeys, each with space for one or two birds. Some cages have pointed roofs and are known as chalets; those with rounded tops are called domes, and are also sometimes referred to as pavilions.

Architectural cages, as their name suggests, are miniature replicas of various buildings ranging from Gothic churches, castles and pyramids, to oriental palaces and pagodas. In the thirties, they took on impressive proportions, even imitating skyscrapers. They could house dozens of birds and were so big that their use was mainly confined to orangeries.

Outdoor cages and aviaries were usually made of metal, which was painted to delay corrosion. Sometimes the cages rested or were hung from metal stands that brought them up to eye level.

LEFT

Designs from the Nouveau Dictionnaire de la Vie Pratique *(Hachette) for metal bird cages for sale in 1923. (top) A dome and (bottom) a two-storey chalet.*

ABOVE

From the same catalogue, a double dome design for two birds, and a single chalet.

Grav. 632. — Volière.

ABOVE
Design for a large aviary abutting a wall, suitable for the grounds of a grand house.

TOP AND BOTTOM, LEFT
Small, wood-framed cages designed to hang on a wall or fence.

TOP RIGHT
Decorative cages were placed on verandas or balconies. Often made from rare woods, they were prized – and still are today – for the intricacy of their design.

TIP
Birdcages were not designed to be left outdoors. If you want to keep yours in good condition, take it inside in bad weather. Some people, however, feel that rust makes old cages more attractive and happily leave them out all the year. When restoring a birdcage, the first thing to do is to wash it gently but thoroughly with soapy water. Removing rust is a tedious job, but well worth the effort. Rub down affected areas with fine glasspaper, then apply clear wax, or, if you intend to leave the cage outside, give it one coat of anti-rust preparation followed by two of an oil-based metal paint.

TOP
An attractive aviary with a handsome zinc cupola. The scalloped frieze lends it an oriental look.

BOTTOM
A bird-fancier's arrangement of cages on a wall has the delightful effect of studied disorder.

OPPOSITE
Many estates still have a dovecote. This example is designed like a small house, with wire netting for walls. Some designs reproduce architectural details of the owner's house.

OVERLEAF
An elegant traditional dovecote made from wood.

nesting boxes, birdbaths and feeders

The idea of fixing nesting boxes to a tree to encourage birds into the garden is a fairly recent one and as well as shelter you will need to offer your visitors food and water. If you consider the box as architecture in miniature, you can indulge any fantasy you like, and you can come across some really kitsch examples of mini-palaces, copies of 1950s architecture, and designer creations to set collectors drooling. It appears to be a scientific fact, however, that birds prefer the more rustic types that blend into the garden. This is why so many nesting boxes are made of plain wood or small branches (especially chestnut), which shed their bark with the sun and rain. Topped with a thatched roof, they look like a country cottage. Earthenware nesting boxes, imitating the mud nests of house martins, can be set under the eaves of the house and woven seagrass roosting pockets provide shelter in winter. You will also need a feeding table, especially for the winter months. Basically all this entails is a platform on a stand with a roof to keep the rain off the food – think of it as a tiny house without walls.

Birdbaths can have two functions in a garden. As well as providing the birds with water, they can act as a decorative element where there is no other water feature. The traditional type is a shallow bowl mounted on a low column. But obviously any shallow watertight container will do – a large shell, an old stone gutter, an urn, vase or redundant basin – anything placed in a reasonably quiet spot where the birds will feel at ease.

ABOVE
A pair of blown glass water-dispensers.

BOTTOM
This wooden nesting box, with a pair of lovebirds on the roof, is full of character.

OPPOSITE
Simple roosting boxes can be made of straw or wickerwork; nesting boxes can be hollowed out from a log or branch; ideal for encouraging tits to nest in your garden.

OVERLEAF
Set in the greenery, these two birdbaths offer our feathered friends somewhere to take a drink and preen their feathers.

ATTRACTING THE BIRDS

For small birds like blue tits, an entrance 25 mm/1 in wide will
suffice. Open fronted boxes will attract robins and wrens.
Nesting boxes and feeders should be sited in a quiet spot and
out of reach of cats.

Clean nesting boxes thoroughly each year, after making sure the
birds have left the nest first. Throw away the old nest and clean
inside with a stiff brush. Wooden boxes should be treated with
an eco-friendly preservative.

scarecrows and bird-scarers

A scarecrow, the farmer's stand-in as guardian of the crops and terroriser of birds, is a down-to-earth, ephemeral creature, usually patched together out of any materials to hand. His ancestry may derive from Ancient Egypt, where farmers fixed nets on wooden frames to keep the birds off their fields. The Greeks used wooden effigies armed with a sickle or a cudgel, while the Romans preferred statues of a god surrounded by offerings that had a double purpose, to keep the birds away and win the god's favour for a good yield. In Germanic countries, the effigy was of a witch who was burned after the harvest. In Japan, the traditional bird-scarer consists of fish scales and pieces of glass and metal fastened to a stake.

The traditional scarecrow in England and France is the dummy figure fixed to two crossed poles and dressed in straw-stuffed rags and an old hat. There is a hint of other more sinister figures about him – carnival giants and ogres from fairy tales, perhaps.

Other bird-scarers are devoid of any human resemblance, such as tin cans threaded on string, which rattle and bob in the wind, or objects like metal balls, mirrors and brightly coloured papers that flash as the sun catches them. The final category is altogether grimmer – a dead crow nailed to a stake in the middle of the field.

But all sorts of whimsical designs are in order, and anyone can make a scarecrow – children, adults and even artists.

TOP OPPOSITE AND OVERLEAF LEFT
Mere scarecrows they may be, but the ones shown here come in highly imaginative designs. They may be ephemeral but nonetheless they are attracting interest from more and more artists.

OVERLEAF RIGHT
Another way of protecting young salad crops from the birds is to cover them with willow cloches.

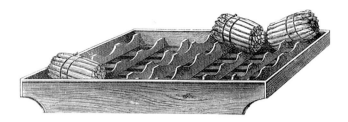

TOP
Wooden rack for draining asparagus.

basketry

OPPOSITE
Drying trays and baskets for fruit, grapes or vegetables are still everyday items; they're also in great demand as decorations in country dwellings.

TIP
To clean basketwork, dust down, then wipe clean with soapy water, avoiding detergents. Rinse and leave to dry. Finally, apply linseed oil but do not varnish. Commercial products are available to protect the material from woodworm. Don't leave basketwork in the sun. If you use a basket to display plants or flowers, use an inner watertight container which can be concealed with moss or twigs – or line the inside of the basket with a piece of thick plastic roughly sewn in place.

Basketwork brings back fond memories of the past. Willow has great visual appeal, with its fine, golden brown coloration and variety of weaves. It is light, durable and authentically rustic. It is a genuine product of the countryside and it harmonises perfectly in the garden.

There are a number of ways a gardener can make the most of baskets. You can plant them up and fix them to a wall, hang them from a tree, or arrange a small collection along the top of a low stone wall.

Basketry probably dates from Neolithic times; the oldest pieces to be discovered – in a remarkable state of preservation – have been in Egyptian tombs. In Europe, the craft was practised throughout virtually the whole countryside, with each region adapting its designs to local needs. Thus, on the coast the main output was lobster cages and creels for fish or shells, and in vine-growing areas baskets were made to be carried on the backs of grape-pickers as well as wicker holders for bottles and demijohns.

It was the abundance and cheapness of the raw materials that made this large-scale production possible. The type of willow that grows in damp areas was the first choice both for country folk, turning out items for their own use, and for professional basket makers. But baskets could also be made from hazel, buckthorn, bramble – proof against parasites and vermin – straw, clematis stems, couch grass, reed and so on. Pedlars then hawked the products around the countryside. There was also a demand for much larger items made from basketry, especially for storage or transport, such as fruit baskets, and cages for hens or young calves.

The modern industry produces beehives, flat baskets for cut flowers, lidded versions for strawberries, racks for drying fruit and dog and cat baskets. There is also a demand for decorative domestic articles, and for very fine work that can involve splitting the strands into thin sections.

COLLECTING TIP
As clematis and couch grass are no longer used commercially in basket making, any object made of these two materials is probably old. In the case of other materials, like willow, older pieces are on the whole more finely woven than newer ones. Restoration is very costly, so look for items in good condition. Nevertheless, some patched up and repaired baskets have an undeniable charm.

BELOW
A column of revolving shelves used for storing fruit.

Grav. 457. — Fruitier pyramidal.

tools

The earliest tool made by Man, dating back to Palaeolithic times, was a piece of flint, which was sometimes fixed to a branch to give it a handle. As the early nomads settled and became farmers they developed tools to work the land. The Ancient Egyptians made use of a form of hoe, with a double-pointed branch fastened to a handle. The Greeks owned hoes, fruit-picking hooks, rakes and wooden spades and shovels, implements that the Romans improved on by adding metal reinforcements. In the tenth and eleventh centuries, Crusaders returning from the Holy Land brought back tools made of iron, horn or bone. In the Renaissance, tools became more sophisticated, lighter and, above all, more widespread. Thus, in the seventeenth century, the diarist, John Evelyn, could publish an inventory of 70 items. This list would be extended in the next hundred years with new inventions, some linked to the cultivation of exotic species imported from the New World or Asia.

Until the 1800s, most tools were made by blacksmiths to individual customers' orders. But then, under pressure from a new middle class with a passion for gardening, they began to be mass-produced. Catalogues of the time advertised several hundred items, each carefully described and attractively illustrated.

Tools may be divided into several categories, according to whether they are designed for preparing the soil, sowing, planting, harvesting, grass-cutting or pruning vegetation.

For heavy preparatory work, the pick and shovel were the two main implements traditionally employed. The former has a metal head fixed to a handle, with one end pointed, the other flattened, and is used to break up hard surfaces. How deep it penetrates depends on its quality and the skill with which it is wielded. Its complement is the shovel. With a flat metal blade attached to a shank, it can also be used to dig with, but its primary function is for lifting and moving earth.

Two other tools are used for maintenance – the spade and the hoe. The spade has existed since the Iron Age and was originally used to till the fields. It has since become a garden implement and consists of a handle with a metal blade in one of several possible shapes, and maybe a footrest allowing the user to apply more pressure. It serves to turn over the earth, dig trenches, plant trees or cut neat edges along borders.

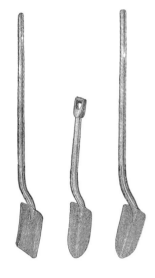

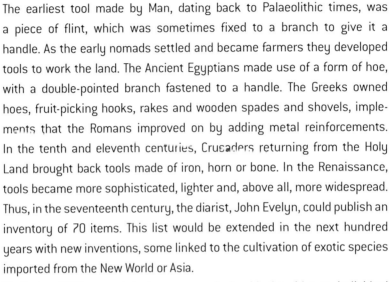

LEFT
Three types of shovel from the Dictionnaire de l'agriculture *(Hachette) published in 1900.*

TOP
Bellows for fumigating from M. de la Vergne.

OPPOSITE
Basic gardening tools, such as hoes, forks and spades, have altered little over the centuries.

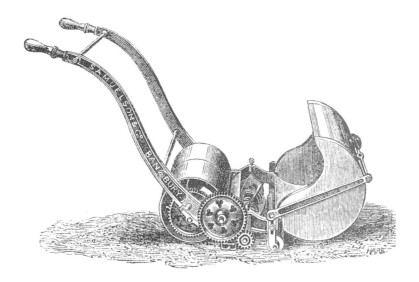

TOP
Lawn mower made by Samuel & Co.

BOTTOM
Lithograph of accessories from the chapter called Gardening *from a book entitled* The Four Seasons *published in Paris, 1850–60.*

Hoes have also been around since the Iron Age. A wide variety of designs exist, some for specific purposes and crops, such as vines or potatoes, but basically the hoe has a small blade, with a space between it and the long handle. It is pushed back and forth through the top layer of the soil, breaking it up and removing weeds. From the eighteenth century, the draw hoe became indispensable for the weeding of parks and gardens, used in conjunction with hand-held grubbers and weeders, some equipped with claws.

Rakes, already in service in Roman times, also come in an assortment of designs. They can be used to break up small clods, level beds, remove weeds, stones and root material or to collect leaves, cut grass and debris into heaps.

A dibble is a single pronged implement for making holes for seeds or seedlings. Planters also exist for bulbs, potatoes, etc. For positioning and lifting small plants, gardeners use a hand trowel. For transplanting and pricking out, some people design their own little tool.

For trimming small trees and shrubs the gardener has recourse to a pruning knife, which will cut almost anything. Its handle may be curved to give a better grip and the curved blade ends in a point. Since the 1600s, folding blades have been the norm, turning the device into a pocket knife. Sometimes the handle is fashioned out of a quality wood like ebony or box.

OPPOSITE
(top left and bottom right) Garden tools illustrated in The Four Seasons *(see opposite).*
(top right) Rubber stamps for labelling seed packets.

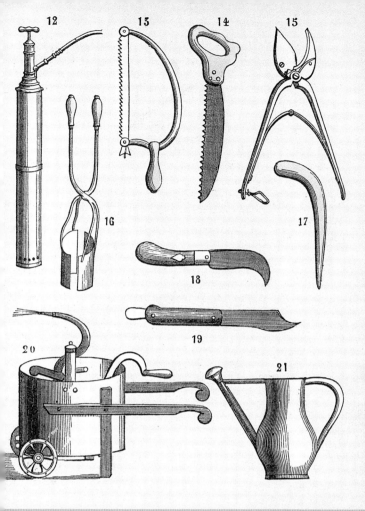

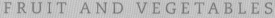

FRUIT AND VEGETABLES

Very specific tools have evolved for growing and harvesting various fruit and vegetables. There are special hoes for onions, beet and cabbage hooks, salsify forks and asparagus knives. A fruit-picker, invented around 1750, has a metal or wooden basket on the end of a long pole designed to reach the fruit at the top of the tallest branches.

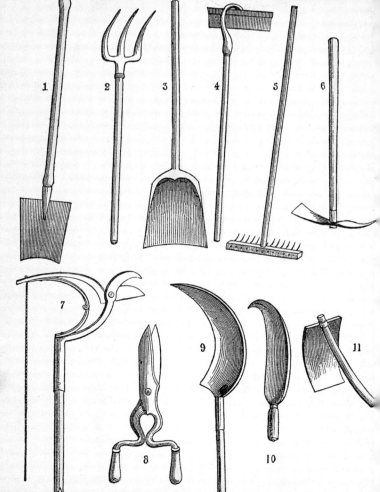

COLLECTING TIP

The most interesting tools are one-offs, hand made by a labourer or craftsman. Old implements, even if very worn, fetch much higher prices than new ones. Authentic, period repairs add value, but beware of modern copies – some of these imitations are poorly balanced and may have decorative motifs which make them hard to hold.

A rival to the pruning knife arrived on the scene in 1897 when the Marquis de Molleville invented secateurs. They proved to be a hit and soon many versions were available, suited to specific tasks and users – special ladies' versions, for instance. Then came the long-handled pruner for reaching otherwise inaccessible branches. Based on a pair of secateurs, and resembling a parrot's beak on a long pole, it was worked remotely by wire. In fact a wide array of shears, knives, trimmers, saws, slashers, hooks and loppers were developed to deal with vegetation and branches. Tools became very specific for their tasks – for example budding knives and bark-strippers.

TOP AND BOTTOM,
Spring in the orchard: pruning fruit trees (top). Summer: watering (bottom). Illustrations from The Four Seasons, *by Belin and Bethmont, Paris, 1850–60.*

TOP AND BOTTOM
Autumn: harvesting fruit and preparing beds (top). Winter: protecting tender specimens with straw; preparing manure for the hothouse; lagging greenhouses and cold frames (bottom).
Illustrations from The Four Seasons, *by Belin and Bethmont, Paris, 1850–60.*

Before the advent of modern machinery, cereal crops and hay were harvested with scythes and these were also used to control grass and weeds in gardens. Scything was a backbreaking job, and the worker had to sharpen the blade several times a day. The sickle, a smaller curved implement, was used to cut the edges of the field.

Pitchforks were used in the fields at hay-making and harvest to lift corn sheaves and hay bales on and off wagons. The modern multi-tined garden fork is also used to lift large plants and weed clumps, as well as to break up heavy soil. Small, hand forks are suitable for weeding round plants and maintaining greenhouse beds and nursery areas.

OVERLEAF
Barrows, baskets, tools and tender plants, like the olive sapling, need protection over winter.

cloches and greenhousess

At one time the greenhouse and the cloche would have been tucked away in the walled vegetable garden and no one would have looked twice at them. Now, like the watering can, they have taken on a new role in our gardens as decorative features.

Glass bell cloches, designed to protect or force vegetables, evolved from cones made of straw or willow and perforated terracotta or wood covers. It was in the 1700s that examples in blown bottle glass first appeared, with or without a knob. Shapes were varied to suit the plants. Tall, tubular designs for cucumbers, low and wide for melons or cauliflowers. They were hand made, the glass blower using his mouth to shape them, and some reached 60 cm/2 ft in height and width. The chemical composition of the glass affected its colour; it might be bluish, verging on green, or with a slight pink tint. Production ceased after the Second World War.

Lantern cloches had a similar purpose to bell cloches. They are, to all intents and purposes, greenhouses in miniature. Sheets of glass were fitted into a metal frame with putty, with one pane left removable for ventilation. In summer, the glass was traditionally whitewashed to protect young plants from the sun.

In nineteenth-century England, tiny portable greenhouses were quite the fashion, made in a variety of architectural styles. People placed them on their windowsills and, protected from the cold, the plants grew rapidly, screening the interior of the house from prying eyes.

OPPOSITE
Cold frames and cloches were traditionally whitewashed in summer to protect the young plants from the sun.

TOP RIGHT
Two types of windowsill greenhouse once very popular in Britain and Germany, from the catalogue of Dick Radclyffe & Co., Erfurt.

BOTTOM
Lantern cloche with a ring for hanging or carrying.

Glass bell cloches were blown by mouth and the button or knob on top was formed when the glass-blower removed excess molten glass. Today, some Eastern European countries still manufacture these jars, but they lack the craftsmanship and variety of shapes that make the old ones so delightful. Nonetheless, they are useful and decorative items. Watering cans dating from the 1800s can be found in antique shops, though many will have lost their roses. Earlier eighteenth-century versions, however, are real museum pieces.

LEFT
Ideally, every gardener should own a greenhouse for storing frost-sensitive plants and pots over winter.

OPPOSITE
(top) Glass bell cloches for forcing vegetables have become purely decorative items.
(bottom) A wooden crate covered by a home-made cloche made from metal rods bent to shape with wire to hold the sheets of glass.

watering cans

In ancient days, water was stored in tanks, cisterns and wooden tubs and carried in goatskin bladders or leather gourds. The first watering pots appeared around the sixteenth century in Normandy. They were a sort of earthenware urn with a pierced base and, though cheap, they were heavy when filled and fragile. It was not long before sheet iron with its greater durability replaced earthenware and watering pots underwent a change of shape. Instead of being pierced at the base they were made with a pipe which ended in a large, fixed rose. They had a single or double handle and sometimes had their own little cart. The term watering can began to be used during the 1700s and in about 1750, the removable rose was introduced and copper superseded sheet iron. In the late 1800s, watering cans were mass-produced in zinc, tin and tinned or galvanised iron, and nearly all of them were round or oval.

wheelbarrows, carts and trolleys

An old handcart overflowing with vegetation, or flower-filled terracotta pots nestling in a discarded metal barrow – features like these can add a country look to the most urban of gardens or brighten up an otherwise unprepossessing corner.

The Chinese are reputed to have invented the wheelbarrow. In the West, the first pictorial representation occurs in a twelfth-century illustration of cathedral building. The barrow initially had two wheels, reduced to one before the 1600s, when it was used to transport merchandise. Some illustrations show itinerant vinegar-sellers with casks on their barrows.

In country districts, it was the cartwright's job to make anything that had wheels, from a farm wagon to a carriage, and, of course, sturdy handcarts, trolleys and barrows. The wheelwright's speciality was the making of the wheels. He would use local woods – oak, for its strength, acacia because it was flexible, as well as elm, fir, ash, beech and horn-beam. The result was a great assortment of vehicles, ranging from large-wheeled handcarts for fetching timber from the forest down to trolleys, milkmen's carts, flower-sellers' barrows, labourers' barrows with steel linings, garden barrows and carts used to transport stones, branches and even coffins.

In the nineteenth century, wood was superseded by metal and the manufacture of barrows transferred from the craft workshop to the factory. Heavy-duty models were mass-produced in metal for farms and building sites and lightweight versions for gardens.

TOP

This old wooden cart, still an impressive piece of work, has found a last resting-place in a garden.

LEFT AND BELOW

Designs for a barrow for transporting liquid manure, a garden barrow, a fodder barrow and a porter's trolley. All from the Dictionnaire de l'agriculture *published by Hachette in the late nineteenth century.*

Fig. 751. — Brouette de grenier.

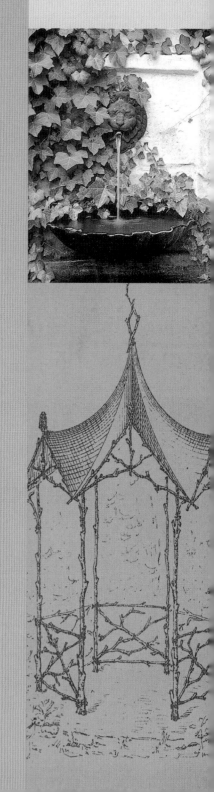

garden buildings

statues

obelisks and stone balls

architectural elements

weather vanes and roof ornaments

Ornamental
features

animal sculptures

garden gnomes

fountains

garden buildings

Almost every major garden boasts little ornamental buildings that catch the eye and arouse the visitor's interest and admiration. Set at the end of an alley, where paths intersect, or in some secret nook just waiting to be discovered, they are intimate, shady and cool; a place of refuge and a place of protection from a sudden shower. Ideal for meditation or the exchange of confidences, they afford the gardener moments of tranquillity. For centuries they have also given architects the chance to indulge their fantasies.

Long ago, the Greeks and Romans equipped their gardens with areas of shade in the form of pergolas or small porticoes. In some of the Pompeian frescoes it is possible to see latticework pavilions that break up the monotony of long paths. Renaissance Italy, ever harking back to classical times, mimicked their splendours with imitation grottoes and loggias. The kings of France, in the seventeenth century, sought refuge from the pomp and splendour of the court in little country-style pavilions and half-timbered cottages. In the 1800s, wrought iron structures came to the aid of those middle-class garden owners who did not want wooden pavilions in rustic or gothic style. Garden buildings were not confined to the West. The Chinese attach symbolic significance to these garden structures where they come face to face with the two vital elements of the universe, mountains and water. The Japanese, too, love pavilions set in water-gardens.

Kiosk, pavilion, temple, belvedere, summerhouse, chalet and gazebo – the list of terms used for architectural structures found in gardens is very confusing, especially since they are used quite loosely. A temple, of course, is easily recognised with its classical, circular structure of columns and a chalet or cabin is, as one might expect, a small wooden building. The word gazebo is said to be a jocular derivation from the word gaze plus the Latin suffix *ebo* meaning 'I shall gaze', since it is open at the sides and designed to give a view of the garden or landscape. A belvedere is more or less identical, deriving from the Italian *bel* meaning beautiful and *vedere*, to see.

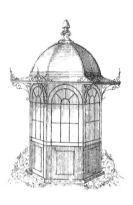

ABOVE

Small wrought-iron garden kiosk from the Pantz à Pont-à-Mousson *catalogue produced in the early 1900s.*

TOP

A year-round refuge, this wooden cabin keeps out the cold, but its many windows allow the occupants to keep in touch with nature.

ABOVE

Designs for mock grottoes and hermitages for English gardens, from a print collection of 1776–83.

Both are frequently sited on a vantage point like a hill or mound. The French term *gloriette* is sometimes used when referring to garden structures found in France, the word being based on *glorie*, meaning splendour in Old French. From the sixteenth century, the word described a small, hexagonal, open-sided structure, with a tiled or thatched roof resting on a set of stone or iron pillars, surrounded by a low wall, trellis or balustrade.

A kiosk – a term more often used today to describe a small freestanding shop selling ice creams or newspapers – derived from the Turkish *koshk* which in turn derived from the Persian *kushk*. This structure was highly popular in Elizabethan gardens, and during the eighteenth and nineteenth centuries proliferated in a wide variety of materials and decorative schemes, particularly those of exotic origin. In France, under Napoleon III, three versions rivalled each other in popularity – the Moorish, the gothic or Swiss chalet, and designs revealing Japanese or Chinese influences.

If the gloriette and kiosk were freestanding and open-sided, the loggia was not. Built into, or abutting, a wall, it was a cloister-like shelter originating in Italy, supported at the front by pillars, with or without arches. As for an arbour, this is not really a building at all, but a shady retreat whose frame is partially covered with vegetation.

A grander construction is the pavilion, a word that comes, via the French, from the Latin *papilio* meaning butterfly. The Crusaders brought back the custom of using tents as garden shelters, and some suggest that the name came from the curtains that closed the entrance to the tent resembling butterflies. The design was resurrected in the 1700s, but this time the painted canvas was supported by a frame of metal stakes, or it could be made from metal panels painted to look like a tent. At the same time, the word came to mean a structure where people could sit and play cards, take tea or listen to chamber music. Some were large enough to put up guests or even to lodge a mistress. By the nineteenth century, the term had also come to mean a temporary tent at a country fair or a small freestanding building.

Finally, we have the summerhouse. Though the word is now used indiscriminately to denote a whole range of garden structures, it differs from those already described by being a truly enclosed building. Its value lies not in the view it affords but in its privacy and tranquillity. In the eighteenth century it also became an outlet for the fantasies of the architect or owner of the property and in its extreme form it might be numbered among the whimsical extravaganzas known as follies. A century later, it was more likely to be a craftsman-built affair, sometimes masquerading as a fairy-tale cottage made of wood and moss.

OPPOSITE

(top and bottom left) These old gypsy-type caravans have abandoned the road to make delightful cabins or children's playhouses. (bottom right) The heart-shaped cut-out in the door, fretted roof edging and soft colours make all the difference to this wooden cabin.

OVERLEAF

(left) A fairytale rustic cottage of simple wooden construction – the sort of place where young girls turn into princesses and pumpkins into carriages. (right) Slender stone pillars and a wrought-iron roof give an airy lightness to this gazebo.

TIP

All garden buildings need to be protected against the weather. Clean wooden structures thoroughly and apply an eco-friendly wood preservative. If parts have already started to rot – look for dark stains or soft patches – replace the damaged section with new wood. Minor damage can be treated using a proprietary wood hardener. Ironwork structures should be treated similarly to metal furniture (see pages 74 and 79).

CABIN OR CARAVAN?

Whether you want to play Robinson Crusoe or simply have somewhere to store your tools, there's nothing like having a little hideaway at the bottom of the garden. You can try building one yourself with a few planks or some salvaged materials. If you visit a salvage yard you may find you have quite a choice — rustic versions, like those once used by hunters or foresters, outbuildings from farms or horticultural businesses, old garden sheds, and huts from building-sites. Why not mount them on an old hay wagon? Gypsy-style caravans are also very popular but quite rare.

statues

In ancient times, statues were extensively used to represent the higher powers. Egypt had her divinities and sphinxes and Greece her own gods and heroes. It was the Greeks who were the first to use sculpture in their gardens, lending them an ornamental value in addition to their symbolic significance. Thus the approaches to academies and gymnasia were lined with mythological figures. The Romans imported Greek statuary, from which they were inspired to represent their own pantheon – Neptune, Mercury, Venus, Hercules, Jupiter and a range of goddesses who presided over the cycles of nature and the arts. Early on, they discovered the art of positioning statues, the best example of this being at Hadrian's Villa near Rome. Yet it was not until the Renaissance that garden statuary really came into its own. Fascinated by Ancient Rome, Italian princes and their entourages of architects and artists studied classical ruins and collected antiquities which they then displayed in their own gardens. At the Villa d'Este, for instance, there are pieces that the owners removed from Hadrian's Villa. This era of flourishing creativity also produced original works in marble, alabaster and stone depicting grim pagan divinities, monsters, nymphs and fauns. They were often arranged in large numbers along balustrades and terraces, bordering waterfalls and fountains or encircling parterres.

But it was probably in seventeenth century France that the use of statuary in the garden reached the height of perfection, even if the subject matter was lacking in originality. Not only was the technical quality exceptional, but it also played a major part in the very architecture of the garden, providing focal points and controlling the symmetry, balance and harmony of the surroundings. One of the finest examples is the central *allée* at Vaux-le-Vicomte leading from the chateau to the great gilded statue of Hercules, its entire length lined with sculptures, obelisks, urns and basins. The majestic layout of the gardens at Versailles is also breathtaking in this respect, with its grand perspectives punctuated by innumerable statues, the result of the collaboration between garden designer, Le Nôtre, and sculptor, Le Brun. Versailles had a considerable influence throughout Europe and even in Russia, where one of Le Nôtre's pupils, Charles Le Blond, architect to Peter the Great, played a leading part in designing the famous gilded statues for the summer palace at Peterhof, near St Petersburg.

The English tended to go their own way. They did not feel the same attraction for marble, which they considered too sophisticated, preferring lead for its alluring patina and because it lasted better in their damp climate. From the 1700s, lead statues were moulded and mass-produced. Lead lent itself admirably to the pastoral and rural themes which the British adored. In their gardens nymphs, milkmaids, shepherds with their animals and huntsmen figured strongly in the repertoire. Later the Victorians, great lovers of the Renaissance, plunged back into the past and reproduced the urns, statues and obelisks they so fervently admired in Italian gardens. From the end of the nineteenth century there was still a rich output of statuary, though of smaller dimensions to suit the restrictions of space in the gardens of the middle classes.

LEFT
Skilful positioning has produced the perfect partnership between sculpture and plants. This marble Bacchic figure appears to be gently supported at the ideal height by two sections of box hedge. The strong symmetry is softened by the semi-circular curve over the figure's head.

obelisks and stone balls

OPPOSITE
Stone balls flanking flights of steps serve to structure space and guide the eye towards the horizon.

TOP
(left) Sculpted stone pine cones, even if really weather-beaten, can still look good.
(right) Eighteenth- and nineteenth-century garden designers made considerable use of carved geometrical ornaments in formal gardens. This decorative fantasy was conceived by a sculptor of talent.

RIGHT
Finials in the shape of a stylised flower have been in use since the Middle Ages, especially on gables or balustrades.

Placed as talismans beside the temples of Ancient Egypt, obelisks served to ward off the forces of evil. They were omnipresent in the days of the Greeks and Romans and reappeared in the decorative repertoire of Renaissance and baroque designers. They also occurred in relatively large numbers in eighteenth-century English gardens, as can be seen at Chiswick House in London. Very tall, they were intended to catch the eye at a time when the boundaries between the garden and the surrounding countryside had disappeared. In France, they became fashionable again under the Directory, when there was a passion for everything Egyptian. In a miniaturised form of about 1 m/3 ft tall, they proliferated in gardens, either in pairs when they would be used at the top of a flight of steps, or in rows lining a walk or a terrace.

Another symbolic ornament was the globe, a timeless representation of both the Earth and the Universe. Roman emperors, like many European sovereigns after them, adopted it as their emblem, surmounting it with a phoenix, eagle, dove or, in the case of Christian monarchs, an angel or a cross. In the nineteenth century, its simple, perfect shape made it popular for use in the garden. Like the obelisk, these balls may be set in pairs to flank an entrance or in rows along an esplanade or terrace, in which case they are likely to be mounted on a stone base in the form of a pyramid or cube. The globe is traditionally carved from stone, although examples are occasionally seen in latticework, perhaps supporting a climbing plant.

COLLECTING TIP

As well as pyramids, balustrades and stone balls, a large number of empty pedestals, bases and steles can be found in antique shops and architectural salvage yards. What ornaments they once carried no one will ever know, but even on their own, they make artistic garden features. Also worth looking out for are boundary stones.

TOP

Anything can be turned into a garden ornament, even a simple piece of cement pipe, here set amongst a clump of hostas.

OPPOSITE

(top left) A striking contrast of materials: a metal armillary sphere on a grand stone plinth.
(top right) Another old stone pedestal: this one supports an urn planted with lavender.
(bottom) Two square troughs accentuate the symmetry in this Provençal garden.

architectural elements

COLLECTING TIP

With the modern taste for mixing styles and eras, gardeners are always on the lookout for all sorts of ornaments, including fragments of capitals, columns, pillars, arches and vaulting from neo-classical temples. It is also possible to turn up more unusual items, like window surrounds or dog sculptures.

It was in the gardens of Ancient Rome that temples and porticoes inspired by Greek architecture first made their appearance. One of the finest examples is the Canopus at Hadrian's Villa. During the Renaissance, enlightened patrons with a love of antiquity commissioned buildings based on classical designs, such as the Rometta of the Villa d'Este, with its grottoes and *nymphaea*. The taste for classical architecture reached its peak in the romantic gardens of the 1700s. The whole of Europe, and England in particular, was smitten with a passion for colonnades and rotundas. For proof, we need only to look at the Temple of Friendship in the Schönbusch Park in Bavaria or the columns in the gardens of Aranjuez near Madrid. But the most perfect examples are to be found in England with the classical temple at Barnsley House near Cirencester and the Palladian series at Stowe Park in Buckinghamshire.

The Renaissance also gave birth to a new, poeticised view of ruins — ambivalent symbols of paganism, dead, yet deathless. This taste began to find expression in the seventeenth century, notably in painting, and was encouraged by the excavations at Pompeii, Herculaneum and Segesta, though its noblest interpretation appeared a hundred years later in the archaeological romanticism of the artist Piranese. In France, Hubert Robert, steeped in Italian culture, not only painted imaginary ruins and real temples side by side, but also adopted the same approach in his garden commissions. A Temple of Filial Piety and a copy of Trajan's Column share the grounds of the Château de Méréville. At the Château d'Ermenonville, the Marquis de Girardin designed a romantic garden where the mock ruins of a Temple of Philosophy rubbed shoulders with a column dedicated to Contemplation. At Monceau, Louis de Carmontelle erected an Egyptian pyramid, a colonnaded *naumachia* and a ruined fort, all in the same eighteenth-century landscaped garden, on to which, in 1861, Jean-Charles Alphand superimposed an English-style romantic layout.

OVERLEAF

(top left) A fine staircase winding round a fountain set in a niche; the curving ramp, the balustrade and the sculpted urn are all vital to the final effect.
(bottom) A seventeenth-century wall-mounted stone sundial.
(top right) This corner of a salvage yard contains a collection of boundary stones, urns and a sculpted bouquet awaiting a buyer.
(bottom) A double flight of steps with elegant, uncluttered balustrades allows the pool and the view beyond to be admired from above.

SUNDIALS

Before the invention of modern instruments, water clocks and sundials were the sole means of telling the time. The first known sundial goes back 5,000 years to Ancient Egypt. The Tower of the Winds in Athens had several flat dials mounted vertically, and at Pompeii, spherical versions have been discovered. Others were conical and even portable. At the start of the sixteenth century, clocks began to rival dials, but were so inaccurate that the dial remained in use for another 300 years. Many examples are set horizontally, with a flat disc mounted on a pedestal and a pointer called a gnomon. The disc is set parallel to the horizon, and is engraved with hour markings — the twenty-four meridians arranged according to a calculated perspective. The shadow of the gnomon indicates the time. In the case of upright and sloping versions, the hour divisions are laid out in such a way as to rectify the effect of perspective, but the gnomon still points in the direction of the Earth's axis.

BALUSTRADES

Generally speaking, balustrades appeared during the Renaissance. Many European gardens were constructed on terraced slopes, which made it possible to create some very spectacular designs uniting broad perspectives with a series of descending levels. Balustrades flanked the staircases connecting each level and fronted the terraces. The balustrade also played a role elsewhere in the garden, guarding against dangerous overhangs, indicating the best viewpoints and forming a demarcation between the finite limits of the garden and the wider vistas of the landscape beyond.

weather vanes and roof ornaments

The origin of the weather vane may lie in the standard a victorious general hoisted over a captured city to proclaim his conquest. As well as announcing his identity, it indicated the direction of the wind. However, the material rapidly deteriorated, and in the twelfth century the Vikings, it is believed, invented the metal standard, which fulfilled both functions. Owners soon began mounting these on their castles to remind the world of their importance.

Early wind vanes were relatively simple and consisted of a lightweight plaque revolving on a pivot. A cross denoted a Crusader, initials a nobleman and, on a church, the cockerel was both a reminder of Peter's denial of Christ and a pre-Christian symbol of vigilance. In some countries the use of a weather vane was restricted to the nobility and the clergy, by law.

Until the mid-1800s, weather vanes were custom made by hand, in the same way as trade signs and plaques. The various metal parts were cut out manually, hammered on a special wooden structure, then welded and polished. Later the individual pieces were cast in moulds for mass production though the construction remained the same, and weather vanes were manufactured in batches and sold by mail-order catalogue. Some included the letters for north, south, east and west to make it easy to determine the direction of the wind.

The figures found on weather vanes vary considerably and common examples include Old Father Time with his scythe, a ploughman and his team of horses, a hunter and his dog, or a horse and carriage. Sometimes they served as trade signs for craftsmen like carpenters, coopers, tinsmiths and blacksmiths. Farm animals formed another major theme. Motifs changed with the times, and trains, cars and planes appeared in

OPPOSITE
The cockerel is a symbol of Christianity. Metal versions dismantled from churches sometimes turn up as garden features.

LEFT
An entertaining little summerhouse attached to the main building. Note the purely decorative wrought-iron finial forming the centrepiece of the scalloped roof.

LEFT AND RIGHT
These highly elaborate finials and zinc roof ornaments are crying out for a place in a garden.

deference to progress. There is a French joke that weathercocks make easy targets for hunters returning empty-handed!

Finials and roof ornaments are placed at the very end of the roof-ridge where the roof timbers meet at the king post, or over the hip-ends of mansard roofs, set at the places most vulnerable to rain to prevent water from seeping into the rafters. They are found on castles and churches as well as houses, from the humble to the very grand, on roofs made of many different materials.

Roof ornaments can be as simple as an upside-down urn, but the tendency has been to create highly crafted and decorated artifacts, to the point that they became a distinguishing mark akin to a coat of arms. In France, every region has its own styles, some of the most remarkable hailing from Burgundy, Normandy, Périgord, Quercy and the Beauvaisis.

Finials and roof ornaments were individually hand-made until the nineteenth century. They could be sculpted like bouquets of flowers or take the shape of a cone or pyramid, maybe surmounted by a ball. Some indicated the profession of the house-owner, in a manner similar to weather vanes and trade signs, or they reproduced his favourite animals. Various materials were used but lead-covered iron, terracotta, earthenware or zinc were the most common.

In the 1800s, the manufacture of these items was mechanised along with the tile industry. Like weather vanes, they were sold in large numbers and began to feature in mail order catalogues and eventually they were turned out on an industrial scale in factories.

TIP
If you come across a period weather vane, clean it, gently removing any rust, and apply a protective agent. As far as possible, avoid major restoration or re-painting.

animal sculptures

Since the dawn of civilisation, animals, both real and imaginary, have been used to symbolise gods, heroes and desirable qualities. The Egyptians, who regarded the forces of nature as divine, portrayed Hathor, goddess of joy and love, as a cow, Horus, the sun god, as a falcon, and Anubis, the god of death, as a jackal. Sphinxes – lions with human heads – guarded places of burial. For the Assyrians, the lion and the bull were metaphors for good and evil. Greek mythology teems with fabulous animals like the winged horse Pegasus. The Greeks began sculpting animal figures from the late ninth century BC, mainly horses, deer and birds of prey. In the Roman and Greek pantheon, each god or goddess possessed an animal attribute: Jupiter had his eagle, Juno a peacock, Minerva an owl and Diana a fawn. Horses and rabbits, cockerels and ducks, fish and pigeons are also recurring themes in Roman sculpture.

In Christian art, God is symbolised by an assortment of animals including the lamb, deer, peacock or fish, and in the legends of the Middle Ages, unicorns, sphinxes, griffins, centaurs and sirens existed side by side with more familiar creatures like sheep, rams and cows. Renaissance artists returned to ancient themes and allegories. Baroque gardens were peopled with monkeys, frogs and Tritons. Animals – domestic, wild or fabulous – besieged the grottoes and the pools. In the seventeenth and eighteenth centuries, animal art was closely linked to the popular sport of hunting. Favourite subjects included stags at bay, dogs and riders pursuing deer, wild boars and wolves or lions turning on horses.

From the nineteenth century, interest in animals increased. Artists worked with major foundries and the resulting sculptures were sold internationally. Some restricted themselves to native or domestic creatures such as hens, sheep, squirrels, frogs and woodland birds. Others preferred the company of the mythological – centaurs, fauns or Maenads, and were at their happiest depicting Io's heifer, Orpheus' tortoise or Athene's owl. The final group limited their interest to wild beasts, subjects that received an added impetus from the colonial exhibitions of the inter-war years.

COLLECTING TIP

From majestic lions to metal frogs and earthenware geese, the subjects and materials used for animal sculpture are legion. Try to hunt down an original, keeping a watchful eye out for modern copies, though these usually display telltale signs. Some copies of older works date from the 1800s. It's worth thinking about reconstituted stone, which is cheaper than the real thing, and there are good quality items to be had.
A considerable number of bronze reproductions of animals are made in Britain including hares, bulldogs, cats, ducks and geese. Bronze cranes, symbolising longevity, are an important element in Chinese and Japanese gardens. Genuine versions are assembled from several parts, but copies from Thailand are produced in one piece.

OPPOSITE

(top left) A stone frog, perfectly placed beside a pond.
(top right) A stag's head in the style of a hunting trophy looks quite at home on this garden seat.
(bottom left) The artist captures a cast-iron hare with its young in characteristic pose.
(bottom right) Plants will happily scramble over these animal shapes made from dried moss.

OVERLEAF

(left) Forest animals also came to live in a garden.
(right) Glass bell cloches, balls, and an old stone stoup make an attractive still life arrangement.

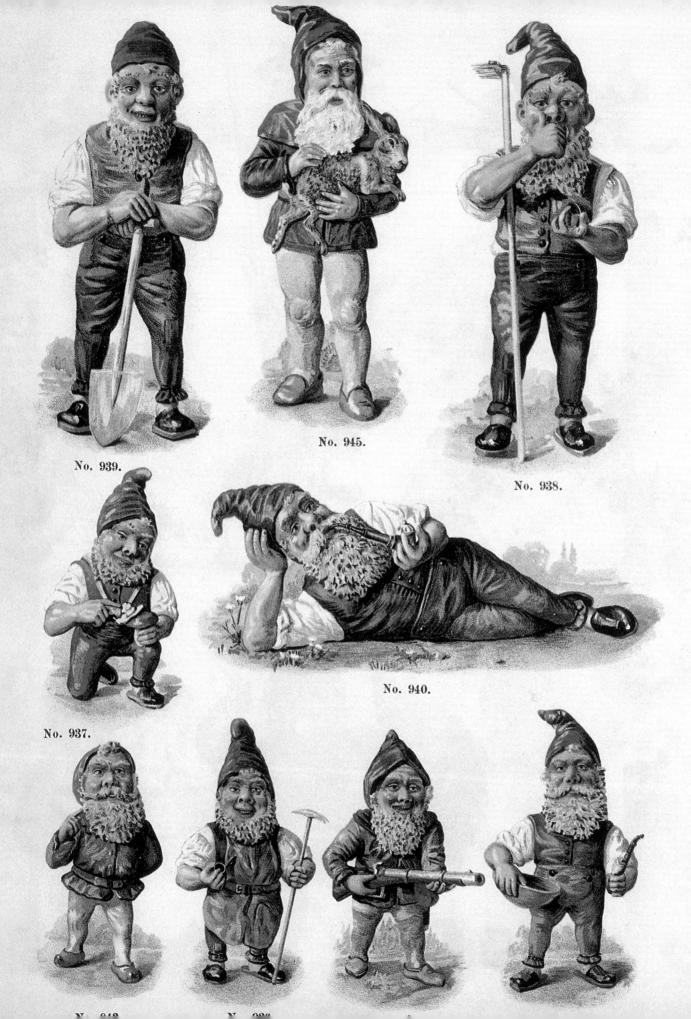

No. 939.

No. 945.

No. 938.

No. 937.

No. 940.

garden gnomes

Garden gnomes have a twofold ancestry. The first is a character from Greek mythology, Priapus, the misshapen offspring of Aphrodite and Dionysus, who was abandoned by his parents and became the god of the garden. The second is linked to German and Scandinavian folklore and the tales of Odin and Thor. The dwarfs, it was said, lived underground, where they excelled in metalwork – particularly helmets and swords – and working with precious stones. One day, however, they emerged into the daylight and set themselves up in the forests. They toiled hard to make a living, becoming masons, carpenters, potters, shoemakers and the like. Finally, they invaded our gardens.

The first small figures of garden gnomes appeared in Germany in the mid-nineteenth century. The man who established their popularity was August Heissner, who set up a business producing glazed earthenware figures at Gräfenrod in Thuringia, in 1872. His venture prospered and, in the 1920s, Heissner began to export on a large scale, particularly to England and the United States, including California. Walt Disney was said to have been intrigued by the figures and his film *Snow White and the Seven Dwarfs* made them familiar to children the world over.

Originally, it took two weeks to make a ceramic figure; today, it can be done in eight minutes using PVC. The modern Heissner catalogue illustrates over 200 designs and each figure is moulded, baked, cooled and then spray-painted. Other major firms have sprung up in Silesia, Eastern Europe and France, but in Asia, the Czech Republic and Poland a large number of imitators producing poor quality gnomes have jumped on the bandwagon. Garden gnomes are also made in stone or in wood, most of the wooden

LEFT

Ancient and weather-beaten, this humble gnome has got the autumn blues; all he can do is sweep away the dead leaves.

ones coming from the forest regions of Central Europe. Every gnome is different, each with his own character, facial expression, clothing and accessories. Gnomes often come with some distinctive sign of their trade, favourite sport, hobby or to celebrate a special occasion, like Christmas. Manufacturers are quick to update them with allusions to fashionable trends and, of course, they have their pets with whom they share their activities. But the business has become too profitable to stop there and a whole range of accessories is available for your gnome's comfort and amusement. You can buy houses, windmills, wells, cars, carts and even spaceships.

Gnomes are highly popular in Germany, where they have set up home in one garden in every two, but they can be found in England, Canada, South Africa, Brazil, almost anywhere you care to name. France, Spain and Italy seem less besotted with them. Nevertheless, kidnappings and campaigns to Free-the-Gnome regularly provide them with excellent publicity.

OPPOSITE

(top left) Garden gnomes with chubby children's faces and beards seem to be gradually sinking into the ground!
(top right) The ancestor of the garden gnome is, perhaps, this marble dwarf from Salzburg, made around 1715.
(bottom left) Gnomes, as everyone knows, love celebrations, especially with music.
(bottom right) A genial gnome with his fishing rod introduces a touch of humour to the edge of a pool.

BELOW

In this miniature universe things are not always made to scale – a snail can be as big as a well or a pelican.

fountains

OPPOSITE
Deep in a garden, an old fountain built into a low stone wall provides water for potted plants.

In Ancient Greece, fountains were considered sacred to the naiads or water nymphs. When Alexander the Great conquered Persia, he discovered a series of bewitching gardens whose influence soon spread to the West, and the fountain gradually shed its religious connotations to become a purely decorative feature. In the gardens of Roman villas, fountains were either installed against a wall in a kind of niche flanked with sculptures and mosaics, or mounted on pedestals. In the enclosed gardens of the Middle Ages, as seen in contemporary illustrations, the fountain, whether a simple pool or a relatively major sculpture, was the only decorative element. Set in the middle of the garden, it was an invitation to sit and meditate.

Some of the most prolific fountain builders of all time were the Arabs. Their skill was prompted by the necessity to make the most of the tiniest trickle of water. Their fountains formed the central element of highly symmetrical gardens and a marble basin was set either on the ground, or on a plinth in the middle of a pool, where paths or rills intersected. When the Arabs invaded North Africa in the seventh century and Spain a hundred years later, they brought their unique art form with them. The results can still be seen in the magnificent Alcazar gardens in Seville and most notably in the Lion and Myrtle Courts of the Alhambra.

The art of the Italian fountain designers was at the opposite end of the spectrum, but by no means less extraordinary. In and around Rome and Florence, where the water supply was abundant and there were plenty of skilled engineers to exploit it, the whole explosive spirit of the Renaissance

TOP
Water splashes merrily from a rusty tap shaped like a dog's head.

BOTTOM LEFT
An old pump which would have been a common sight in villages and gardens a century ago.

BOTTOM RIGHT
A simple fountain made from a flagstone and a weathered trough.

TOP

A stone fountain forming the centrepiece of a small pool is sufficient to create a feeling of coolness.

OPPOSITE

(top left) This old stone fountain, set in a niche, is an integral part of the building.
(top right) Water descends from one pool to another through the mouths of winged dolphins; mythological creatures beloved of the Renaissance and often found in grottoes and fountains.
(bottom) An original wall-fountain where the water pours out of the lion's mouth into a shell, from which it overflows into a semi-circular basin.

COLLECTING TIP

Eighteenth-century fountains can be tracked down at some specialist antique firms, but they will be expensive. Many fountains are reproductions, often from the 1800s when there was a lot of copying, or from more recent copies. The deciding factors on price are design, craftsmanship and materials. Some reproductions are excellent, others really rough. Watch out for very soft stone that deteriorates rapidly. A tip for spotting artificial patina – it will be all over the artifact, including the wrong places such as underneath. Some nineteenth-century cast-iron models bear the foundry's stamp. Architectural salvage companies may be able to supply well heads, cisterns, bathtubs or stoups that you can convert into fountains.

seemed to burst forth in the powerful jets leaping skywards from the Terrace of the Hundred Fountains at the Villa d'Este, the immense cascade tumbling down the staircase of Caserta's royal palace and the fountains and mirror-like pools of the Villa Lante at Bagnaia.

French gardens lacked the prolific water resources available to their Italian counterparts, and the terrain was seldom suitable for multi-level terracing. The tendency was for tranquil pools fed by a large network of canals. Nonetheless, the pools were brought to life by numerous fountains, with the accent placed on designs that delighted the eye and the ear simultaneously. At Versailles, a small army of architects, hydraulic engineers and sculptors laboured for fifty years on Le Nôtre's scheme for the gardens and their water features. In 1689, there were so many fountains that it took a day to walk round them. Many derived their inspiration from Apollo, the sun god, whom Louis XIV had adopted as his personal symbol. However, the water supply at Versailles was always insufficient, and it was impossible to activate all 1,400 fountains at once. When the king walked in the gardens, the technicians turned them on and off as he passed.

In the latter half of the eighteenth century, water appeared in the garden in the guise of mountain streams, waterfalls and natural pools, with fountains now considered somewhat *passé*. But they made a comeback in the early 1800s, more popular than ever, in that eclectic mixture of styles and allusions to the past which characterised the century. Catalogues advertised neo-Egyptian or Etruscan-style models, Moorish fountains, classical fountains and rustic fountains. Every type of material was pressed into service – cast iron, lead, bronze, zinc, marble, stone and reconstituted stone. Mass production became the order of the day and this is still true today, but since the Second World War there has been a re-emergence of individual models designed by artists.

sources of traditional artifacts

Antique and junk shops

Reclamation and architectural salvage companies

Demolition and building firms

Auctions; country house or farm sales

Several TV channels have regular gardening and home-making programmes which may suggest ideas and sources

Advertisements in local newspapers and specialist magazines: lifestyle/home-making/antiques/collecting/gardening/county and country life, etc.

Garden centres (these will mainly be reproductions)

Markets, car boot/garage sales, tag sales, estate sales

Horticultural shows and exhibitions (mostly reproductions, but good information available)

Talk to anyone altering/renovating property on your street; do they want to sell something?

Firms are also likely to be listed in Yellow Pages and trade directories.

For a list of architectural salvage merchants, connect to: **www.salvoweb.com**

for antique dealers: **www.bada.org**

There are also hundreds of individual business entries on the web. Try, for instance: **www.architectural-heritage.co.uk** or **www.gardengateco.com**

Again, experiment with entering phrases like 'architectural salvage', 'garden treasures', 'garden antiques', 'garden bygones' or 'reclamation firm' in your search engine.
(Don't forget to put inverted commas round words to be kept together.)
Adding a district or town will narrow it down locally, e.g. **Norwich + 'antique fountains'.**

Most search engines and Internet providers have on-line shopping directories with categories like antiques, gardening, etc.

For reproductions, similar searches are likely to be fruitful: enter keywords like 'reproduction garden ornaments', 'reproduction oil lamps', and so on. Start by visiting
http://www.debbysgardenlinks.co.uk/furniture.htm or
http://www.emilysplants.com/links/gardendecorating.html

bibliography

Christopher, Thomas and Van Sweden, James. *Architecture in the Garden*, London, Random House Publishing Group, 2003

Israel, B. *Antique Garden Ornament*, New York, Harry Abrams, 1999

Jekyll, G. *Garden Ornament*, Woodbridge (UK), Antique Collectors' Club, 1982 (reprint)

Lusty, W. & Sons. *History of Lloyd Loom*. Contact W. Lusty & Sons Ltd., Hoo Lane, Chipping Campden, Glos. GL55 6AU, England (Tel: +44 1386 841333; Fax: +44 1386 841322; e-mail: enquiries@lloyd-loom.co.uk)

Morris, A. *Antiques from the Garden*, Woodbridge (UK), Garden Art Press, 1996

Outwater, M.Y. and E.B. *Garden Ornaments and Antiques*, USA, Schiffer Publishing, 2000

Outwater, M.Y. *Antique Garden Tools and Accessories*, USA, Schiffer Publishing, 2002

Paul, A. and Rees, Y. *The Garden Design Book*, London, HarperCollins, 1991

Plumptree, G. *et al. Garden Ornament: Five Hundred Years of History and Practice*, London, Thames and Hudson, 1998

Rees, J. and Van der Werff, R. *Miller's Garden Antiques*, London, Mitchell Beazley, 2003

Stuart, D. *Classic Garden Features*, London, Conran Octopus, 2000

Symmes, M. *Fountains: Splash and Spectacle . . .*, London, Thames and Hudson, 1998.

Wilkinson, E. and Henderson, M. *Decorating Eden*, San Francisco, Chronicle Books, 1992

acknowledgements

The publishers extend their thanks to all who have assisted in the production of this book and, in particular, Inès Sarramon, whose patience and kindness have been never-failing.

We are also grateful to those antique dealers from the Saint-Ouen markets who kindly put their treasures at the disposal of Christian Sarramon; also to Bertrande de Ladoucette, organiser of the Salon de Viels-Maisons, and to the exhibitors at the Salon Art du Jardin.

Christian Sarramon is deeply appreciative of the generosity shown by those who have made him so welcome in their gardens over the years, especially: Louis Benech, Safia Bendali, Élisabeth Bourgeois, Jean-Jacques Bourgeois, Élisabeth Brac de La Perrière, Sir Terence Conran, Madame Cruze, Dominique Deniau, Mireille Dasana, Michel and Christine Guérard, Arend Jan van der Horst, France Loebb, Olivier Massart, Chris O'Byrne, Hervé Thibault, William Thuillier, Christian Tortu, Fabienne Villacreces; also Jean-Michel Gelly, who graciously lent several fine artifacts from his collections.

All the photos in this book are by Christian Sarramon, except:

© Marie-José Jarry and Jean-François Tripelon: 21 (b), 25 (t), 35 (c), 40 (t), 44, 75, 78 (t), 81, 83 (br), 99 (tr), 103 (t), 107, 117 (tr), 123 (b), 127, 129, 130 (tl), 145 (bl), 148, 153 (bl), 154, 156, 157, 161 (tr).

© Vincent Motte: 45 (b), 49 (b), 60 (b), 65 (t), 150 (b), 179 (br).

© Jean Vigne: (Bibliothèque Municipale de Versailles): 9 (b), 38 (b), 152.

© AKG Paris: 134 (b), 135 (tl, br), 136, 137, 174; © AKG Paris/Heiner Heine: 177.

© Bridgeman Art Library and Bridgeman Library: 36 (t), 41, 61 (cl, cr), 70 (tl), 73 (c, b), 84 (b), 95 (b), 102, 103 (br, bl, bc), 106, 140 (t).

© Kharbine-Tapabor: 16, 27 (tl, br), 48 (tr), 74(b), 79, 82, 84 (t), 85, 86, 90 (tr), 91 (b), 94, 96, 98, 101 (c), 105 (b), 112 (tl), 113, 114, 115, 147 (b), 149 (b), 151 (r).

© Leemage/Costa: 37 (tr), 117 (br), 131 (b), 132 (t), 134 (t); © Leemage/Gusman: 177 (tl, br, bl); © Leemage/Selva: 145 (br).

© M.A.P. 34, 120-121, 124; (c)M.A.P./Nour; (c)M.A.P./Yann Monel: 125.

© Photothèque Hachette: 30, 38 (t), 116, 131 (t), 132 (l), 144, 146 (bl, br).

Supervising Editor: Odile Perrard
Art direction: Sabine Houplain and François Huertas
Layout: Shirley Leong-Ho
Proofreader/Copy Editor: Cécile Edrei
Photoengraving: Aps/Chromostyle (Tours)

First published in the United States of America in 2004
Rizzoli International Publications, Inc.
300 Park Avenue South
New York, NY 10010
www.rizzoliusa.com

First published by Editions du Chêne, an imprint of Hachette-Livre
43 Quai de Grenelle, Paris 75905, Cedex 15, France
Under the title *Dans les jardins de nos grand-mères*
© 2003, Editions du Chêne
Language translation produced by Translate-A-Book, Oxford
English Translation © 2004 Octopus Publishing Group Ltd, London

Printed in Singapore by Tien Wah Press
ISBN: 0-8478-2608-2
Library of Congress Catalog Control Number: 2003098267